Charles Frederick Johnson

English Words

An Elementary Study of Derivations

Charles Frederick Johnson

English Words
An Elementary Study of Derivations

ISBN/EAN: 9783337276157

Printed in Europe, USA, Canada, Australia, Japan

Cover: Foto ©Thomas Meinert / pixelio.de

More available books at **www.hansebooks.com**

ENGLISH WORDS

AN

ELEMENTARY STUDY OF DERIVATIONS

BY

CHARLES F. JOHNSON

PROFESSOR OF ENGLISH LITERATURE, TRINITY
COLLEGE, HARTFORD

NEW YORK
HARPER & BROTHERS, FRANKLIN SQUARE
1891

Copyright, 1891, by HARPER & BROTHERS.

All rights reserved.

PREFACE.

This book is written primarily for use as a text-book in high-schools and colleges. Its object is to call attention to the literary values of words as far as can be done in a brief examination of derivations. It is hoped, therefore, that it may not be without interest for that large class who, though in no sense specialists, take an interest in the history of words, and that some young men may be prompted by it to take up the study of our language seriously.

My acknowledgments are due to Messrs. G. P. Putnam's Sons for permission to insert the tables of Latin and English derivatives from Professor Marsh's lectures, and to the Open Court Publishing Company of Chicago for permission to make some extracts from Max Müller's latest lectures.

To my colleague, Dr. Samuel Hart, I am indebted for many valuable suggestions.

Professor Skeat has been relied on as an authority in etymology.

C. F. J.

TRINITY COLLEGE, HARTFORD, *July* 29, 1891.

CONTENTS.

CHAP.		PAGE
I.	THE IMPORTANCE OF LANGUAGE	1
II.	THE RELATIONSHIP OF THE ENGLISH LANGUAGE	13
III.	NATURE AND PROOF OF LINGUISTIC RELATIONSHIP	23
IV.	SOURCES OF MODERN ENGLISH WORDS	36
V.	ENGLISH WORDS DERIVED FROM CELTIC	46
VI.	CLASSES OF LATIN DERIVATIVES	56
VII.	ARTIFICIAL CHARACTER OF THE LATIN ELEMENT	68
VIII.	LITERARY CHARACTER OF THE LATIN DERIVATIVES	81
IX.	MINOR SOURCES OF ENGLISH WORDS	96
X.	METHOD OF THE WORD-FORMING INSTINCT	113
XI.	GROUPS OF WORDS WITH A COMMON ROOT	129
XII.	ERRONEOUS DERIVATIONS	140
XIII.	ODD AND DISGUISED DERIVATIONS	155
XIV.	GEOGRAPHICAL NAMES	170
XV.	SURNAMES	194
XVI.	WORDS OF THE PROFESSIONS AND TRADES	216
	ADDITIONAL WORDS FOR ILLUSTRATION	244
	INDEX OF SUBJECTS	249
	INDEX OF WORDS AND EXPRESSIONS EXPLAINED	252

ENGLISH WORDS.

CHAPTER I.

THE IMPORTANCE OF LANGUAGE.

WE find ourselves in possession of a very complicated and delicate instrument which we are constantly using even when we are asleep. It is called language, and the first fifteen or twenty years of our lives are spent in learning to use it in a very feeble and imperfect way. If any educational process goes on during the rest of our lives, its result is shown principally in increased readiness and dexterity in the use of language. Language, indeed, is so closely related to character that, setting moral distinctions aside, the manner of using it is what chiefly distinguishes one man from another, and the power of acquiring it is what distinguishes a man from a beast. We naturally use the word "dumb" as a synonym for stupid, and when we say "dumb beast" we instinctively refer to our belief that the power of speech implies what we call reason. Homer calls the human race "articulately-speaking" or "'word-dividing' mortals." The later Greek philosophers, with a sense that the two things were closely related, used the word *logos* for both speech and reason.

In the proposition that the manner of expressing thought in words or language is the criterion of intellectual character, we must be careful to note that the term "words or language" has an extended meaning, for deaf and dumb men who cannot use or hear vocal sounds at all are as certainly intellectual beings as are the readiest and most fluent talkers. When we say that the language-power is the mark of a man, we do not mean the power of vocal utterance, but the power of attaching any note or mark to an idea in the mind, whether that note be a sound, or a gesture, or a scratch on paper. In that broad sense deaf and dumb people use language as truly as do talkers. Even those unfortunates who are deaf, dumb, and blind can, after infinite pains, be given a language through the sense of touch. The fact that until this is done their minds remain absolutely isolated and powerless to form an idea, is a proof of the intimate connection between thought and the means of expressing it. Until Dr. Howe gave the girl Laura Dewey Bridgman an equivalent for a word, she dwelt in blackness and remoteness, substantially without the power of thought. This may give us some idea of the immense importance of vocal words, since even an imperfect substitute for them can produce the difference between rationality and apparent idiocy.

Again, the second proposition contained in the first paragraph, that the power of language is the criterion of human beings as distinguished from brutes, implies another restriction of the usual meaning of the phrase, "the power of language." For beasts possess a certain kind of language-power in great perfection. Their calls of affection or warning to their young, and their notes of defiance, or rage, or pain, are very emphatic and expressive, and are readily understood even by men. But the call of the mother-bird, or the growl of a dog, is not language in the scientific sense. These sounds all express emotion, or are the physical counterparts of certain feelings. They are of the same character as interjections, like "Oh," or "Pshaw," are not in essential nature different from a sigh or a groan, and are no more like real language than is the creaking of machinery for lack of oil. It is words as the sign of thought, not words as the outcome of feeling, that is meant when we say, "No beast has the power of language." Professor Whitney says (*Study of Language*, Lect. xii.): "The essential characteristic of our speech is that it is arbitrary and conventional; that of animals, on the other hand, is natural and instinctive; the former is, therefore, capable of indefinite growth, change, and development; the latter is unvarying, and cannot transcend its original narrow limits."

The language which is the mark of humanity consists of vocal sounds, or their equivalent, attached to mental concepts. Some philosophers hold that without the power of forming the sound, or some equivalent, physical, correlated sign, that we could not even form the concept. However this may be, whether it is true that "without thought no language is possible," or "without language no thought is possible," it is certain that without language there could be no communication of thought, and, consequently, no civilization and no individual development. The question whether language or thought is the primary power is at best a metaphysical one. The two powers are certainly necessary to each other, and there is a quality in one or both which distinguishes man from the beasts. Whether we regard this quality as a radical or an acquired one will depend our fundamental philosophical notions. To the writer it seems a radical quality. It may be instanced that the power of making vocal sounds, and of attaching them to certain concepts, appears in infants with the first ray of consciousness, and that the growth of the power is commensurate with the growth of consciousness. Furthermore, men have been talking to horses and dogs for at least eight thousand years, but neither of those races has made the slightest progress towards acquiring a language. Man, therefore, may be defined as the animal who had originally the power of developing a language, or as the animal who has developed a language.

Since language is so closely connected with human thought, even if not absolutely necessary to it, we can readily see how important the study of words may become. We cannot get hold of a new thought without learning some new words, or at least adding something to the notions grouped about the word we already know, and so enriching and rounding out our instinctive knowledge. On the other hand, to learn something about a word — a thought-implement — ought to enlarge our thought-power by making us more familiar with the implement.

From another point of view, the study of words has a different and perhaps a greater value. It increases our power of enjoyment and our sense of relation to our fellows. The beauty of imaginative literature depends to a great degree on the associations called up by particular words. The use of a word rich in associations in such a manner as to bring out those associations constitutes poetic form far more than does rhyme, or the rhythmical arrangement of accent. These associations —the intimate and poetic meaning of the word— depend to some degree on the history and origin of the word. If the study of words increases, though slightly, our capacity for artistic enjoyment, or even for rational intellectual enjoyment, no further argument for its importance is needed. Indeed, all others may be overlooked.

From the intimate relations between language and thought, from the fact that language is a social product, and the further fact that ruling ideas and methods change from one generation to another, it is evident that language must change also. Entirely new meanings are given to words in the course of time, and sometimes new words are coined which after a while come into general use. Again, many discoveries of new processes or inventions of new devices are made in physical science, for which new words must be found.* That very delicate characteristic, the flavor or literary value of words, changes from century to century, even if the meanings do not change. Some words lose caste, others are promoted into good

---

* The vocabulary of the modern science of Zoölogy is said by the author of the Introduction to the *Century Dictionary* to reach the enormous total of 100,000 words, 60,000 of which are in use in books at present. Probably not more than two hundred of them are in general use.

society. Language is therefore in a continual state of change from the action of several forces. Old words are dropping out and coming under the class marked "obsolete" in our dictionaries. New words are appearing, and, most important of all,* new meanings, sometimes fuller, sometimes more restricted, are slowly attaching themselves to the old words which are retained. If the language were not written, the words of one generation would not only convey entirely different ideas to the next, but they would hardly be intelligible to it, for pronunciation changes even more rapidly than meanings. If any body of men is isolated, their speech soon becomes a dialect, and before many years possibly a new language. It is thus that French, Spanish, Portuguese, and Provençal grew out of the old Roman speech, as it displaced the languages of the conquered countries. Therefore it is usual to say that language is an evolution—that is, a product whose growth is predetermined and regulated by certain laws.

But language is an evolution in a restricted sense, since it follows the evolution of a nation—or its growth in civilization—at a distance, and may borrow much more or much less from some

---

* Compare, for instance, the words "freedom," 'anarchy," "king," "righteousness," "people," "nature," as held now and in the seventeenth century.

foreign language than the people themselves take from any other nation. It is not an evolution as a plant is which grows from a definite seed and goes through certain stages of change till it reaches maturity and then dies, because, if for no other reason, its environment, the thought of the people which moulds it, is itself an evolution of a very complicated kind. The language of a civilized nation undoubtedly changes continually, both in pronunciation and in texture, according to certain laws, but it does not necessarily expand as the civilization of the people grows broader and fuller. Our language, for instance, has accumulated a great many words during the past three hundred years—many more, indeed, than it has lost, but it is not a more perfected instrument than it was three hundred years ago, when Shakspeare began writing his comedies and King James's version of the Bible was made, although it responds to a wider range of thought. When we use the word, evolution, as applied to the growth of a language, we must remember that we use it in a very restricted and metaphorical sense. The importance of a study of words is illustrated by the fact that so many mistakes arise from the careless use of this very useful word, "evolution." For instance, the successive stages through which a language passes are not necessarily stages of development towards a definite and determined end, as the use of the word "evolution" in this connection would imply.

The study of a language falls into two main branches: the examination of the material, and of the way in which the material is put together. The material is words, and they may be considered with reference to their meanings, or to their derivations, or to both. The body of laws which govern the grouping and modifications of words is called grammar. The two branches constitute philology, or the scientific examination of the structure and material of a language as it is at present, and as it was in its earlier stages. When the words and grammar of more than one language are carefully examined, with a view of discovering resemblances or distinctions and bringing them under general laws, if any can be found, the study is called comparative philology, or—especially if the treatment is broad, and language in general rather than some one language in particular is the subject-matter—linguistics. There is also another branch of the general science of language, and that is phonetics, or the examination of vocal sounds, the mechanism which produces them, and the laws and customs which govern the changes in the pronunciation of words in different nations and in different centuries. It has thrown a flood of light on the manner in which words grow, but it is an extremely difficult study, and is the basis of the modern "science of language." This book will deal simply with the immediate derivations of a few groups of English words. Its object is literary, not philological, and it presupposes only the knowledge of Latin that students entering college usually possess.

When it is said that the object of this book is literary, reference is had to the fact that by knowing something of the derivation and history of English words we come to hold them in a fuller and richer sense, and to have a certain number of associations with them which enables us to use them more accurately and more picturesquely. A feeling for words, such as Charles Lamb and Emerson, among others, possessed, is of course a natural gift. But all men possess at least the rudiments of that discriminative sense in words, and it is a sense remarkably responsive to cultivation. The true way to strengthen it is to read good literature, and to note the peculiar and delicate use of words by literary artists. The study of derivations is only an aid to this exercise. If we know the derivation and history of a word we appreciate it more fully, just as we know a man better when we have known him in his youth than if we had first met him in middle age. Thus, when we learn that "precipitate" means to throw one's self headforemost, and that it comes from *præ caput*, the word acquires a life that it had not before. "Dilapidated" is a strong word, but how much more graphic it becomes when we remember that it comes not from *di lapsus* (fallen down), but from *dis* and *lapis*, and is based on the idea of a building where the stones have fallen down in ruin—"not one stone left upon another." We know that it is from *lapis* (a stone), from the *d* in the word. In the same way the derivations of many words throw light on their meanings, and are frequently very suggestive of new uses. All great writers have used words with an unconscious sense of the various accretions of meaning they have received from time to time. The scientific study of language is perhaps the greatest and most fruitful of all the modern lines of investigation. It has secured a great body of facts, and has thrown a flood of light on the historical development of humanity. But only specialists have the time for this, whereas any one can, with the aid of a modern dictionary, examine the history of a large number of words of his own language, and gain some power of using them in new relations. And all persons should do at least as much as this, since words are the tools of all, and not the special property of the philologist.

Before considering the subject of derivations, it will be well, however, to make a brief classification of the European languages, that we may the better understand the position and genesis of our own.

On the question of the origin and growth of language, students are advised to read Max Müller's two series of lectures, entitled *The Science of Language*, and his later book, *Language and Thought*. Professor Whitney's admirable treatise, *Language and the Study of Language*, as well as his shorter book in the International Science Series, *Life and Growth of Language*, should also be read. The most recent German views can be found in the *Introduction to the Study of the History of Language*, by Strong, Logeman, and Wheeler.

CHAPTER II.

THE RELATIONSHIP OF THE ENGLISH LANGUAGE.

The English language is one of an extensive group or stock of languages spoken by the peoples in Europe and Asia, who have had the greatest part in the development of civilization. This is called the Indo-European, or Aryan, stock—Indo-European referring to the territories in which the languages of the stock have been spoken, and Aryan to the original race or tribe from which all or nearly all of those speaking the languages so related are supposed to be descended. By Germans it is usually called the Indo-Germanic stock. These languages are not all related to each other, or to the primitive language, in the same degree, and those which are the most closely related to each other are gathered into sub-groups or branches. No part of the original language has survived, nor is it known where the speakers of the original language lived, nor how long ago they lived. The deduction from the nature of the words that are common to all or nearly all the languages of the stock would point to a locality where barley was raised and where certain trees grow and certain animals could live. It has been usual to refer to the high ground of Central Asia as the home of the original Aryans, or the Proto-Aryan tribe. Other philologists maintain that they came originally from the fertile plain northward of the Black Sea in Europe, and others, even, that the Scandinavian peninsula has the best claims to be regarded as the seat of our prehistoric, ancestral race. That there was an original race there can be little doubt, for there certainly was once an original tongue, and some few facts about its mode of life can be discovered, but the determination of its abode after the lapse of so many centuries is probably impossible. At all events, very wide boundaries must be assigned. It is quite possible, too, that the climate of the Old World may have changed materially since the day of the ancient Aryans, so that the evidence drawn from the names of the trees and plants and animals known to them may not point to any definite locality.*

* As the original language must have developed before political institutions made large empires possible, we may assume that the area in which it was spoken was limited. It is not asserted that all, or even a considerable part, of those now speaking Aryan languages are physical descendants of the Proto-Aryan tribe. Race is one thing, and language quite another. Some races perpetuate their language;

The branches of this great stock known since historic times are as follows:

I. THE INDIAN.—This contains the various dialects of Hindustanee. The principal literary representative of this group is the Sanskrit, which as a spoken language died out some three centuries before the Christian era. It is the speech of the oldest Aryan civilization, and is a very copious and graphic language, and knowledge of it forms part of the education of learned Hindoos even now. Probably as a whole it resembles most closely the tongue of the primitive Aryans, although, of course, the language of a highly intellectual and thoughtful people, like that which wrote in Sanskrit, is far more developed than the speech of their nomadic and semi-barbarous progenitors could possibly have been. The modern representatives of Sanskrit are the Hindustanee and other dialects of Northern India.

II. THE IRANIAN.—This covers the languages of Persia—old Persian and modern Persian. The Indian and Iranian branches of the Aryan stock constitute the south-eastern or Asiatic division. The five other branches constitute the north-western or European division. Its modern representative is the language now spoken in Persia.

others seem to hold it very loosely. In the amalgamation of races the better-developed language survives in a modified form.

III. THE HELLENIC.—This includes Greek, ancient and modern, the most finished, exact, and copious of the Aryan languages. Modern Greek is sometimes called Romaic. As a literary and national language, Greek has enjoyed a longer life by far than any other Aryan tongue.

IV. THE SLAVONIC, OR SLAVO-LETTIC.—This includes Russian, Bulgarian, Servian, etc. Russian, the leading language of this branch, is spoken by many millions of people, and is developing a fine literature. The race is the youngest to enter the community of civilized peoples, and the language is said to be marked by vigor and melody.

V. THE CELTIC.—The languages of this branch are rapidly becoming extinct. The Celts are of very great antiquity, and once occupied France and the British Isles. They were divided into two groups, the *Kymri* or *Cymri*, and the *Gaels*. The tongue of the Cymri is represented by Welsh, Cornish, and Armorican, or Breton, spoken by the peasants of Brittany. Cornish became extinct in the last generation. The Welsh possess a copious imaginative literature, but although their blood has entered largely into that of our people, their language seems to have affected English but slightly. Gadhelic, the second division of the Celtic branch, is represented by Irish, the native language of Ireland; Erse, the language of the Highlands of Scotland; and Manx, the language of the Isle of Man. The Celtic tongues, all of which are dying out gradually, and being replaced by French and English, are probably among the oldest representatives of the great Aryan stock in colloquial use in Europe, unless that distinction be given to the modern representatives of the Italic. Greek is considered to be a younger offshoot from the parent stock than Latin.

VI. THE ITALIC.—The Latin is, of course, the most important of the languages of this branch, which comprised many tongues spoken in ancient Italy. It is perhaps more closely related to Greek than to the Celtic or Teutonic. It is the source of several important modern languages, called as a group the Romance languages. They are the Italian, the Spanish, the Portuguese, the French, and the Provençal. The Provençal, once spoken in Southern France and Northern Italy, developed a highly-cultivated lyrical literature in the twelfth century, but sank to the level of a peasant's *patois* after the political supremacy of Northern France was assured. Of late, successful efforts have been made to revive it. The influence of classical Latin on all of the modern European languages has been very great, since for many centuries it was the language of diplomacy, philosophy, and religion. More than one-half of our English words—though not the more important part—are derived from the Latin, either directly or indirectly, through French or some other Romance tongue.

VII. THE TEUTONIC.—This branch includes English, Dutch, German, Danish, etc. The Italic languages are spoken by about one hundred millions of people, and the Teutonic by not far from twice that number. They have spread very rapidly in the past five centuries. The Teutonic branch is divided into four groups :

1. *Old Gothic.*—This was the tongue of the first of the Teutonic tribes that attained historic importance. They lived in Moesia, on the Danube. A translation of the Bible was made into this language in the fourth century by Ulfilas, a missionary from Constantinople. The Gospels are still extant, and constitute the oldest writing in any Teutonic tongue. The language is extinct, although branches of the Goths were once the rulers of Europe.

2. The *Norse,* or *Scandinavian,* represented at present by Icelandic, Danish, Swedish, and the dialects spoken in Norway, which are slight modifications of Danish, bearing somewhat the same relation to it that Scotch does to English.

3. The *High Germanic.*—This is so-called because it covers the languages spoken by the Teutonic tribes of Upper Germany, *i. e.*, the country up the rivers or farthest from the sea. Old High German dates back to the eleventh century, and

includes the language of the Franks, the conquerors of Gaul, and of the Suabians. Modern High German is what we all know as German, and dates from the printing of Luther's Bible.

4. The *Low Germanic* group, so-called because it was originally spoken by the Teutonic tribes living in Northern Germany. The ancient tongues of this group are Friesic, Netherlandish, Old Saxon, and Anglo-Saxon, or Old English. The Friesic is still spoken on the coast of Schleswig-Holstein. Dutch, or Hollandish, is the modern representative of Netherlandish, and Platt-Deutsch, or Low German—which must by no means be considered a dialect of German, since it is very much more closely related to English and Hollandish than it is to German—is the modern representative of old Saxon. It is a popular idiom, though some modern novels have been printed in it, and is quite extensively spoken. The fourth member of this group is English, which is a thoroughly Teutonic language in spirit and descent, though it has taken up so large a Latin element into its vocabulary. Its grammar is a broken-down Anglo-Saxon grammar, and its articulations are made by Teutonic particles. It has been enriched, not diluted, by words of foreign origin. It is now spoken and read by a larger body of people than is any other language, for Chinese is separated into a large number of dialects, many of which are not intel-

ligible except to the dwellers in limited districts, and the Mandarin, or Court language, is understood only by the educated classes.

As philological science advances, under the guidance of modern phonetics, judgments as to the closeness of relationship between various languages become modified. Classifications slightly differing from the above have been suggested. One of the latest is found in Brugmann's *Comparative Grammar* (1888). He makes one more main branch, the Albanian, the language of Ancient Illyria, the words of which have been detached by patient study from the mass of intrusive Turkish, Slavonic, and Greek terms which have overwhelmed the modern spoken Albanian.

The Armenian, instead of being ranked under the Iranian branch, is made an independent member, and Indian and Iranian are grouped together to form the Aryan branch.

The Gallic is recognized as a member of the Celtic branch, though all that is known of it is a few words quoted by Latin authors and a few proper names, mostly on coins.

The most important modification is in the arrangement of the Teutonic tongues. These Brugmann divides into Gothic, Norse, and West Germanic. Gothic and Norse (or Scandinavian) are considered to be closely related, and the modern representatives of the latter—Icelandic, Norwegian, Swedish, and Danish—were practically a single language down to the Viking period (A.D. 800-1000). These are also called East Germanic, as opposed to the West Germanic tongues—English, Dutch, Low German, and High German.

The Aryan languages are the only ones spoken in Europe, if we except one or two representatives of the Turanian stock, as Turkish, the Magyar (still spoken in parts of Hungary), the Finnish and Lapp of Northern Russia, and the fragmentary representatives of the Semitic speech scattered over Western Europe. To one Semitic race—the Jews —we owe our religion, and to another—the Arabs of Spain—we owe our rudimentary conceptions of science. From the latter we have received quite a number of words, arithmetical, astronomical, and the like, but our speech is widely removed from theirs. There is, however, in the Pyrenees in Spain and France an interesting survival of a people probably even older than the Proto-Aryans. This is the Basques, a small community still adhering to its original speech, which has no affinity to any of the other tongues of Europe. They represent a little fragment of a prehistoric race stranded in a country which has been overrun by Celts, Semitic Phœnicians and Moors, Italians, and Teutonic Goths and Vandals. They are like the isolated vegetable life of a mountain that has survived geologic changes which have transformed the figure of a continent and left the stunted shrubs and mosses of the earlier era unaffected, but restricted to a limited territory where the newer forms could find no foothold. Linguistically and ethnologically, these Basques are entitled to look down upon Spaniards and Portuguese as recent arrivals, and to consider themselves as the pure-blooded, ancient race. Their language, into which a large number of Spanish vocables has been taken, is said to have little fitness for literary use. Ethnologically, they are called Iberians. They call themselves *Euscaldunac*, and their language *Euscara*. They number 500,000, and retain very many ancient customs and race characteristics. The inhabitants of the south-western part of France also show distinct traces of this ancient blood, notably in Navarre, though the language has long been abandoned. The geographical term *Biscay* is derived from *Basque*.

The question of the original home of the Proto-Aryans must always remain unsettled for want of evidence, and for the same reason will always be a favorite subject of discussion among philologists. Students are recommended to read Taylor's *The Origin of the Aryans*, and the papers brought out by its publication. Also the *Prehistoric Antiquities of the Aryan Peoples* (Schrader and Jevons).

CHAPTER III.

NATURE AND PROOF OF LINGUISTIC RELATIONSHIP.

THE relationship of the Indo-European languages spoken of in the foregoing chapter is a relationship of structure and of material both. We shall consider only the relationship of material—that is, of words. But we must remember that merely finding a word, or even a number of words, in one language naturalized in another is no evidence of a common origin of the two languages. Words may of course be borrowed from any other language at any time. These are frequently retained and become fully naturalized. This is especially likely to be the case when the borrowing people does not previously possess or know the thing to which the word is applied. If the telephone and the steam-engine are introduced into China, the Chinese will probably adopt the words we have invented for names of the parts of the apparatus. But the words for the most evident natural bodies and phenomena, and for the fundamental human relations, and for all common operations, cannot well be intrusive words. Sun, moon, water, man, son, daughter, sky, stars, tree, as well as the verbs to kill, to eat, to strike, to dig, to weave, and many others are very evidently primitive words, as are also the numerals from one to ten; and when we find that the German words *sohn*, *vater*, *mutter*, *tochter*, *stern*, *essen*, *gehen* are very similar to our words for the same things, we say confidently, either German is a sort of English, or English is a sort of German, or they are both changed forms of the same original language. This last is evidently much the most likely supposition, for both languages are subject to change. It has been proved to be true by a variety of arguments. One of the simplest is, that when words appear under altered forms in different members of the same family of languages, the diversity of form is subject to a definite rule. The sounds of the two languages are connected by a law. The differences are not hap-hazard, but are regulated. A certain tendency of pronunciation has worked in one language and another tendency in the other. This consideration enables us vastly to increase the number of words which are evidently related in each language, and to say that the differences are accounted for as not original, but as growths. The resemblances must be accounted for, and they point to a common origin ; and to show that the differences also point to a common origin of the two languages in question is one of the great triumphs of modern philology—the scientific treatment of the words of the Aryan languages. The readiest and simplest illustration of this is to be found in the consonantal reciprocity in cognate tongues, which is expressed in what is known as "Grimm's Law," named after its discoverer, the German philologist, Jacob Grimm. The following statement is taken from Earle's *Philology of the English Tongue:*

"We suppose the reader is familiar with the twofold division of the mute consonants into lip, tooth, and throat consonants in one direction, and into thin, medial, and aspirate consonants on the other. If not, he should learn this little table by heart before he proceeds a step further. Learn it *by rote* both ways, both horizontally and vertically :

	LIP (Labial).	TOOTH (Dental).	THROAT (Guttural).	
THIN	p	t	c = k	THIN
MEDIAL	b	d	g	MEDIAL
ASPIRATE	f	th	h (Saxon)	ASPIRATE

By means of this classification of the mutes,*

* Besides the mute consonants we have the trilled *l* and

we are able to show traces of a law of transition having existed between English and the classical languages. We find instances of words, for example, which begin with a thin consonant in Greek or Latin or both, and the same word is found in English or its cognate dialects beginning with an aspirate. Thus, if the Latin or Greek word begins with *p*, the English word begins with *f*, *e.g.*, πῦρ and *fire;* πρό, πρῶτος, *primus* and *first*. Compare with the Saxon words *fruma, frem*, the modern preposition *from*—which is of the same root and original sense — with *for, fare, forth;* πῶλος, *pullus*, with *foal, filly;* *pellis* with *fell;* πῦξ, *pugnus*, with *fist;* πατήρ, *pater*, with *father;* πέντε with *five;* πούς, *pes*, with *foot;* *piscis* with *fish*, etc.

"If the classical word begins with an aspirate, the English word begins with a medial: *e.g.*, the Greek φ, or Latin *f*, is found responsive to the English *b*. Thus, φηγός, *fagus*, and *beech;* φύω, *fu* (perfect stem of *sum*), and *be;* φρατρία, *frater*, and *brother;* φέρω, *fero*, and *bear*. The Greek θ by the same rule responds to the English *d*, as in θήρ and *deer;* θυγάτηρ and *daughter;* θύρα and *door*.

"If the Greek or Latin has the medial, the Eng-

---

r, the sibilants *s, z,* and *x = ks*, and the nasals *n, m*, and *ng*. The last are also labial mutes—that is, the sound is stopped by the lips. Grimm's Law refers, however, only to the consonants contained in the table.

lish should have the thin; that is to say, a classic δ or *d* should correspond to our English *t*. So it does in δάκρυ and *tear;* δύο, *duo,* and *two;* δέκα, *decem,* and *ten;* δέμω, *domus,* and *timbran* (the Saxon word for *building*); δένδρον, δρυς, and *tree;* *dingua,* archaic Latin for *lingua* and *tongue.* These and all such illustrations may be summarized for convenience' sake in the following mnemonic formula:

T	A	M
𝔄	𝔐	𝔗

In this the letters of the Latin word TAM placed over the Gothic letters of the German word Amt are intended to bracket together the initial letters of thins, medials, and aspirates, so as to represent the order of transition.

"In the use of this scheme, we will suppose the student to be inquiring after the Greek and Latin analogues to the English word *kind.* The word begins with a tenuis or thin consonant, and thus directs us to the letter *t* in the Gothic word *Amt.* Over this *t* we find in the Latin word an *m*, and by this we are taught that the medial of *k*, which is *g* (see Table), will be the corresponding initial in Greek and Latin. Thus we are directed to γεν and *gigno* as the analogues of *kin* and *kind.* The same process will lead from *knee* to γονυ and *genu,* from *ken* and *know,* to γιγνώσκω."*

* Skeat formulates the law of phonetic change more con-

In other words, a Latin thin consonant changes into an aspirate in the corresponding English word, a Latin aspirate into an English medial, and a Latin medial into an English thin, and the reverse is of course true in all these cases, the labial, dental, and guttural quality remaining unchanged. A familiar example of a corresponding phenomenon is that a German or Frenchman invariably changes the English *th* into a *d*, saying *de* for *the*.

"These examples will satisfy the reader that here we have traces of a regular law, and that our language is of one and the same strain with the Greek and Latin — that is to say, that it belongs to the great Aryan or Indo-European family.

"A succession of small divergences which run upon stated lines of variation — lines having a determinate relation to one another, and constituting an orbit in which the transitional movement revolves: this is a phenomenon worthy of our contemplation. It is the simplest conception of a fact which in other shapes will meet us again, namely, that the beauty of philology springs out of that variety in unity which makes all nature beautiful and all study of nature profoundly attractive."

cisely and comprehensively. I give Earle's statement because it is more graphic, and seems to me more likely to impress on the young reader the breadth of the relation.

"It would be easy to discover a great number of examples which lie outside of the above analogy. One important cause of unconformability is the introduction of foreign words. This applies to all Teutonic words beginning with *p*, which are foreigners* and not subject to Grimm's Law. There is also a certain amount of accidental disturbance. Casualties happen to words as to all mortal products, and in the course of time their forms become defaced. The German language offers many examples of this. If I wanted to understand the consonantal analogies which exist between English and the German, I should prefer as a general rule to go to the oldest form of German, because a conventional orthography, among other causes, has in German led to a disfigurement of many of the forms."

Furthermore, it is only in the early stages of a language that words are spelled as they are pronounced, and Grimm's Law is applied to letters. The spelling changes much more slowly than the pronunciation. In fact, after printing becomes general, it is very difficult to change the spelling of words. Thus there have been many changes

---

* That is to say, "foreigners" in the sense of not conforming to Grimm's Law. At least ninety-five per cent. of our words beginning with *p* are derived from Latin or Greek, but a few, *e. g.*, pith, paddock (a toad), pad (in footpad), path, pant, pebble, prick, pride, plough, pod, purr, etc., are of undoubted Teutonic lineage.

in the pronunciation of English during the past century, but the changes in spelling have been comparatively unimportant, and have not followed the changes in sound. We have dropped the *k*, for instance, in words ending in *ick*, like *music* and *mathematics*, derived from the Greek, although the pronunciation of the final syllable has not varied. Fortunately, consonants remain comparatively fixed, but many words containing the vowel sound represented by *ea*, like *sea* and *tea*, have changed from the *a* sound to the *e* sound as represented in *he*, but the spelling remains and will always remain the same.*

Thus, changes may be going on in the pronunciation of a language of which philology has no record.† It is very doubtful if we could under-

* The Irish still retain the early sound of *ea*, and call *tea*, *tay; sea*, *say*, etc. In this and in many other peculiarities of what we call *brogue*, their pronunciation of English is much nearer to that of educated Englishmen of the seventeenth and eighteenth centuries than is ours. Pope makes *tea* rhyme to *away*, and to *say :*

"Muse o'er some book, or trifle o'er the tea,
Or with soft musick charm dull care away."
Again,
"Here, thou great Anna! whom three realms obey,
Dost sometimes counsel take, and sometimes tea."

Still earlier, Surrey makes *praise* rhyme to *peas*, *heat* to *great*, and *peace* to *days*. We have saved this old sound in *great* and *break*. The French words from which *please*, *reason*, *treason*, and *ease* are derived, all have the *ā* sound.

† The decay of the trilled *r* in many parts of our coun-

stand English as spoken by Francis Bacon and his contemporaries. Fortunately, the great characteristics of English were formed long before that date, and therefore stand embalmed in the printed language. If spelling varied as rapidly as pronunciation does, philologists would be very much at sea. The origin of some modern words would have been entirely obscured.

The effect of the discovery of the wide relationship of the Aryan languages has undoubtedly been very great. For a relationship of language implies, though it does not prove, a relationship of blood. Max Müller says that the name Indo-European "marked not only a new epoch in the study of language, it ushered in a new period in the history of the world." In fact, he seems to think that the linguistic bond, evidenced by consonants, vowels, and accents, proves an intellectual fraternity far stronger than any merely genealogical relationship. Blood may be thicker than water, but it does not follow that language is a tie stronger than blood. The strength of the "Panslavic idea," for instance, is based on a feeling of blood relationship, and German national-

try, and the New England tendency to change final *aw* into *awr*, making *law* and *saw* into *lawr* and *sawr*, is another instance of phonetic change. The misplacement of the *h* in England is still more remarkable. No matter how careful an Englishman is to avoid it, he sometimes falls into it if sufficiently excited.

ity rests on the conception of race, not language. It will be best, however, to allow this eminent philologist and entertaining writer to speak for himself. Max Müller says:

"When the Hindus learned for the first time that their ancient language, the Sanskrit, was closely connected with Greek and Latin, and with that uncouth jargon spoken by their rulers, they began to feel a pride in their language and their descent, and they ceased to look upon the pale-skinned strangers from the North as strange creatures from another, whether a better or a worse, world. They felt what we feel when later in life we meet with a man whom we had quite forgotten. But as soon as he tells us that he was at the same school with ourselves, as soon as he can remind us of our common masters, or repeat some of the slang terms of our common childhood and youth, he becomes a school-fellow, a fellow, a man whom we seem to know, though we do not even recollect his name. Neither the English nor the Hindus recollected their having been at the same school together thousands of years ago, but the mere fact of their using the same slang words, such as *mâtar* and *mother*, such as *bhrâtar* and *brother*, such as *staras* and *stars*, was sufficient to convince them that most likely they had been in the same scrapes and had been flogged by the same masters. It was not so much that either the one or the other party felt very much raised in their own eyes by this discovery, as that a feeling sprang up between them that, after all, they might be chips of the same block. I could give you ever so many proofs in support of this assertion, at all events on the part of the Hindus, and likewise from the speeches of some of the most enlightened rulers of India. But as I might seem to be a not altogether unprejudiced witness in such a matter, I prefer to quote the words of an eminent American scholar, Mr. Horatio Hale: 'When the people of Hindustan in the last century,' he writes, 'came under the British power, they were regarded as a debased and alien race. Their complexion reminded their conquerors of Africa. Their divinities were hideous monsters. Their social system was anti-human and detestable. Suttee, Thuggee, Juggernaut, all sorts of cruel and shocking abominations, seemed to characterize and degrade them. The proudest Indian prince was, in the sight and ordinary speech of the rawest white subaltern, only a "nigger." This universal contempt was retorted with a hatred as universal, and threatening in the future most disastrous consequences to the British rule. Then came an unexpected and wonderful discovery. European philologists, studying the language of the conquered race, discovered that the classic mother tongue of Northern Hindustan was the elder sister of the Greek, the Latin, the German, and the Celtic languages. At the same time a splendid literature was unearthed, which filled the scholars of Europe with astonishment and delight. The despised Asiatics became not only the blood-relations, but the teachers and exemplars of their conquerors. The revolution of feeling on both sides was immense. Mutual esteem and confidence, to a large extent, took the place of revulsion and distrust. Even in the mutiny which occurred while the change was yet in progress, a very large proportion of the native princes and people refused to take part in the outbreak. Since that time good-will has steadily grown with the fellowship of common studies and aims. It may freely be affirmed, at this day, that *the discovery of the Sanskrit language and literature has been of more value to England in the retention and increase of her Indian Empire than an army of a hundred thousand men.*'

"This is but one out of many lessons which the Science of Language has taught us. We have become familiarized with many of these lessons, and are apt to forget that not more than fifty years ago they were scouted as absurd by the majority of classical scholars, while they have proved to be the discovery of a new world, or, if you like, the recovery of an old world."

It may be doubted whether the practical humanizing effect of the conclusions of philology is quite as great in overcoming race prejudice as the above quotation would lead us to infer. Their power in broadening the minds of men of education is certainly very great. They should be welcomed and valued as truth without any reference to political bearing. Imperial policy with regard to Turkish alliances or to the government of Hindustan will hardly be influenced by linguistic generalizations. But any sense of the antiquity of our Aryan relationships ought to give us a fuller sympathy with the other civilizations of our stock, and a sounder foundation for our respect for those of our own Germanic branch.

The mutations of vocal utterance in groups of men whereby first dialects, and finally distinct languages, are formed, are subject to a number of laws which modern philology is seeking to disentangle. The article on pronunciation in the *International Dictionary* is as accessible an explanation of the mechanism of human speech as can be mentioned. It contains an admirable, systematic discussion of the action of the vocal organs in forming the sounds of the English language, and opens a branch of the subject to which this book does nothing more than refer.

An Introduction to Phonetics, by Laura Soames, is an excellent analysis of the vocal sounds of English, French, and German.

CHAPTER IV.

SOURCES OF MODERN ENGLISH WORDS.

Various theories have been advanced to explain the origin of language. None of them is altogether convincing, although some are sustained by very ingenious and original arguments. If the origin of language was definitely settled, the origin of the human race would be also settled, and after that the origin of life on this planet would present little mystery. It is much more satisfactory to confine ourselves to historic time, or to the period during which we have written documents, which, indeed, offers a sufficient field for the generalizer and for the accumulator of facts.

Our English of to-day is the speech of a Low-Germanic people, so greatly modified by change as to be substantially a new language compared with its form in the tenth century, and further modified by the naturalization of a very great number of words of a foreign tongue. During the past nine or ten centuries there has never been a period when a generation of Englishmen could not understand the language of their grandchildren, though possibly when the change was most rapid the men of one century might have regarded the men of the next as speakers of a foreign tongue if they could have heard them talk. At the same time, English is an entirely distinct language from Anglo-Saxon. A very rapid review of its stages of growth will enable us to understand better the character of modern English.

The island of Britain was at the date of the Christian era inhabited by Celts, representing both of the great Celtic families: the Cymri and the Gaels, the Cymric tribes occupying the southern half. It was invaded by Julius Cæsar 55 B.C., and subsequently made a Roman province, the work of subjugation extending from A.D. 42 to the close of the first Christian century. The northern part of the island, now Scotland, was never entirely conquered, and savage tribes of Celts—possibly of a still older race—maintained their independence there. When the Roman Empire began to break up, the legions were recalled, and Britain was abandoned early in the fifth century. The Roman invasion left no radical traces on the language of the inhabitants, beyond a few geographical names generally compounded of *caster*, a *camp*, which will be noticed hereafter. It is evident that Britain was never Latinized in the thorough manner that Gaul and Spain were.

Previous to the withdrawal of the Romans, it is highly probable that members of the energetic Low German tribes, who occupied what is now Holland, Schleswig-Holstein, and North Germany on the Baltic, had settled on the eastern shore. At all events, a Roman officer, having command of a number of galleys, was styled "Count of the Saxon Shore,"* and his jurisdiction extended from the Thames as far north as the Saxons would be likely to land. His duty must have been to look after those already in Britain, or to keep others of the active marauders out. The Jutes especially were dreaded as fierce and bold pirates as much as the Northmen were later. But as soon as the military power was withdrawn, the inhabitants of South Britain were exposed to incursions from their savage kindred of the North, and from the Low Germans across the Channel and the North Sea. According to the Anglo-Saxon chronicle, Hengist and Horsa came over in 449 with a body of Jutes —either by invitation of the Britons or of their own motion—and founded the kingdom of Kent. In 477 Ælla landed near Chichester, and founded the kingdom of the South Saxons, or Sussex. During the sixth century the Angles, a closely-

---

* See Dean Church's story, so named, for an excellent romantico-historic picture of this time.

SOURCES OF MODERN ENGLISH WORDS. 39

related tribe, founded kingdoms in the north, the largest of which was Northumbria. The seven kingdoms, Kent, Essex, Sussex, Wessex, Northumbria, Mercia (the *march*, or frontier, or *marked-off* place), and East Anglia—including the modern Norfolk and Suffolk (the North and South people) —are sometimes referred to as the Heptarchy. These invasions of course imply the conquest and subjugation or removal of the Britons, and were followed by bloody wars between the settlements until Wessex and Mercia, under Alfred, attained a precarious overlordship. There is some evidence that the word Angle was regarded as a generic name. At all events, the country as a whole came to be called Angle-land. It may be, however, that the Angles were so far superior in numbers that their specific name was given to the entire country conquered by them and the Saxons.

It must be borne in mind that at that time England was a wild country, large portions of it being covered by unbroken forests and impassable swamps. The settlements were made up the valleys of the rivers or along the old Roman roads. Thus the division into independent kingdoms, as they were called, is accounted for. The Celts were driven into inaccessible places towards the west, and occupied Cornwall, Wales, Cumberland, and Strathclyde. They were called generically Welsh —*i. e.*, foreigners (Anglo-Saxon., *welisc, foreign*).

Cornwall means West Wales; and Cumberland, the land of the Kumroi, or Cymri. Many of the Celts were no doubt reduced to slavery, especially in the large cities like London, or remained in a semi-servile condition; certainly their blood has gone to make up the modern Englishman, although their speech has affected his speech but little.

The Low Germans were hardly settled in their new country when they were themselves subjected to invasion. Their third cousins, the Danes, or Northmen, were as enterprising pirates as the Saxons had been. They landed in their open boats on the coast of Yorkshire and East Anglia, and burned and plundered in their turn. They also made permanent settlements, and their king, Canute, became overlord of England. This historic fact is mentioned because the Danish or Norse language has slightly influenced English. It seems probable that at that time the Danes and Anglians could understand one another's language imperfectly. At all events, there was no difficulty, at a later date, in the reception of certain Danish forms into the nascent tongue. It must be borne in mind also that the language of the different districts of England was different, and that there was a southern, northern, and midland dialect, each of which has left its mark on the agricultural speech of the district where it was originally spoken, the southern dialect being the foundation of the

English we speak. Dialects, if isolated, grow into languages, but in a country under a central government one dialect assumes supremacy as the language of the governing class and of educated people, and the other dialects are relegated to provincial obscurity. Thus Scotland, having been an independent kingdom, there is a marked difference between the speech of Scotchmen and Englishmen, whereas the dialect of Norfolk or Dorset is confined to the lower classes. Particular events having given the supremacy to the Saxons, and London having been the capital, the dialect of the Saxons is the foundation of modern English as spoken by all educated people.

In 1066, England, which had become pretty well consolidated, was invaded by the Duke of Normandy with a large army of men speaking Norman French. He became King of England, and his officers became the local feudal lords of the country. For a period the Anglo-Saxon tongue lost its position as the language of the governing class and of culture. The Christian priests, except in remote country places, used very generally either Latin or French, and one or the other was the language of law and of literature.* The native lan-

* The fact that Englishmen obstinately continued to speak English for two hundred years, so that even those descendants of the Normans who habitually used French were finally compelled to acquire at least a speaking knowledge

guage was of course spoken by the body of the people, but, being under no acknowledged headship, began to change rapidly. Inflections were dropped, and the language approached rapidly its present simple grammatical structure. During the twelfth and thirteenth centuries the course of political events conspired; first, to relieve the Anglo-Saxon from the restraints which a conventional literary standard imposes on a language; second, to bring it back under the yoke after a period of linguistic freedom, and to make it under its new form a strictly national language; third, to reinforce its vocabulary with a multitude of French words. These events were the Conquest, as above mentioned, and the inheritance of a large territory, in addition to Normandy, which the kings of England acquired in France, and then the loss of these Continental possessions, particularly the loss of Normandy, by King John in 1244, after which French civilization ceased to be paramount

of English, is evident from the following quotation from a poem of the fourteenth century:

> "Latyn also y trowe can nane,
> Bot tho that hath hit of schole tane;
> Some can Frensch and no Latyne,
> That useth hath Court and dwelt thereinne.
> And some can of Latyn aparty,
> That can Frensch full febylly:
> And som untherstondith Englisch
> That nother can Latyn ne Frensch,
> *Bot lerde and lewde, old and yong,*
> *Alle untherstondith Englisch tong."*

in England, English nationality reappeared, and the English language took definite shape and assumed the outlines of its present form. Chaucer, who died in 1400, is not only the first writer who is intelligible to us, but the first whom we recognize as distinctly of our own kin in spirit and manner and speech.

From 1060 to 1360 is a long period in the evolution of a language, and to understand the details of the great movement is more than any one not a specialist can hope to do. The changes during this period were so great that we can fairly say that they constitute, not the development of Anglo-Saxon, but the birth of a new tongue. The old speech furnished the skeleton—but even the skeleton was modified—and the most important words, so that the more excited and earnest a man is, the more he tends to use Saxon forms. It furnished also what, for want of a better term, we may call the genius or spirit of the language. This is rather an indefinite expression, but we cannot help feeling that our language is in essentials and manner of growth a Teutonic language, though vastly richer than any other Teutonic tongue, and certainly as far superior in scope and power to Anglo-Saxon as English civilization is to the old Saxon civilization. Of the great number of French words which form part of our language, many are long words expressive of abstractions, and are held in reserve for special service. But, as we shall see hereafter, there are many short French derivatives which form part of our everyday working vocabulary. English is more than a Teutonic tongue into which there has been an infusion of foreign words—it is English. Its characteristic is force. It has its own rhythm quite different from that of Anglo-Saxon. The rhythm, or natural music, is a distinctive mark of a language and probably closely related to the national character of the people who speak it. There is none more varied and vigorous and modern than that of English. It is evident to any one that a truth stated in one language has an entirely different effect if translated into another. This is owing to the great power of form. Language is a form, and as Professor Marsh has pointed out, it has the power of reacting even on him who uses it. One who habitually thinks in French will in time acquire a French coloring to his mind. The importance of knowing something about our language, and of endeavoring to use it in a way conformable to its true character, is very great, because it has this formative power. The use of affected language is not only a sign but a cause of mental affectation. I would not go so far as to say that this malady can be cured by the study of the derivation of words, but at least such study is one means of increasing our respect for our most valuable inheritance—our mother-tongue.

We will now examine briefly some groups of words based on derivations, and also some groups based on the use of various social and industrial classes. The small and comparatively unimportant group derived from Celtic words will claim our attention first, because, with the exception of a still smaller group called "Latin of the first period," it constitutes the oldest addition to the Anglo-Saxon vocabulary from any non-Teutonic source.

CHAPTER V.

ENGLISH WORDS DERIVED FROM CELTIC.

PHILOLOGISTS differ greatly in their estimates of the number of words in English derived from the Celtic tongues. The reasons for this general lack of agreement are: First; Celtic and Anglo-Saxon are both Aryan languages, and when a word is found in one of these languages resembling a word of the same general meaning in the other, the resemblance may be due to the fact that both are descendants from the same word in the Proto-Aryan tongue. Second; the word in question may have been transferred twice, first from the Saxon into the Celtic, and then in its disguised form readopted into Anglo-Saxon, so that what seems a Celtic derivative may from another point of view prove to be a genuine ancestral English word. Third; the paucity of Celtic documents during the period when some interchange of words might have taken place, renders it difficult, by reason of lack of evidence, to decide questions of origin.

As a matter of course, the two races were bitterly hostile, and had little friendly intercourse with each other. The Britons hated the Saxons as invaders, and the Saxons despised the Britons as a conquered and inferior people; nor are these racial feelings entirely eradicated on either side at the present day. But the displacement of the Britons by the Saxons and Angles was a slow process, extending over at least two centuries, and some intercourse must have taken place in the intervals of war. Indeed, in one instance a body of Britons acted as the allies of one tribe of the Angles in their quarrel with another.

Before saying anything about the few words which we have undoubtedly borrowed from the Cymric or the Gaelic branches of the Celtic tongue, it will be as well to notice that every spoken language embraces minor divisions or subvarieties. Thus Max Müller distinguishes four kinds of English. He says:

"There is one kind of English which is spoken in Parliament, in the pulpit, and in the courts of law, which may be called the *public*, the *ordinary* and recognized English.

"The *colloquial* English, as used by educated people, differs but slightly from this Parliamentary English, though it admits greater freedom of construction and a more familiar phraseology.

"The *literary* English, again, requires still

greater grammatical accuracy, and admits a number of uncommon, poetical, and even antiquated expressions which would seem strange in ordinary conversation.

"The *dialectic* English is by no means extinct. The peasants in every part of England, Scotland, and Ireland, though they understand a sermon and read their newspaper, both of which are written in ordinary English, continue to speak their own language among themselves, a language full of ancient and curious expressions, which often throw much light on the history of classical English. These dialects have of late been most carefully examined, and this is a branch of study in which everybody, if only he has a well-trained ear, is able to render most valuable assistance.

"Lastly, in discussing special subjects we are driven to use a large number of *technical, foreign*, and even slang expressions, many of which are quite foreign to the ordinary speaker."

It is evident that there are many subdivisions under each of the above heads. The ordinary English is much the same all over the country at any one period, but differs greatly in different generations. Lord Ashburton's communication and Mr. Webster's reply are made up of about the same class of words, but a State paper or a sermon of the seventeenth century contains many expressions which we now recognize as antiquated.

The *colloquial* English changes much more rapidly, and varies, not only in successive generations, but in different parts of the country. In particular it differs widely in this country and England to-day, and should so differ, since in each it has its own principles of growth. Colloquial English reflects national character, and if national character is individual, it, too, must be individual. If national character is imitative and second-hand, then imported phrases and words will mark colloquial expression.

Literary English changes much more slowly, and does not, or at least should not, vary in different localities, for a writer must have at least some acquaintance with the entire vocabulary of his period, and must read the literature of his time wherever it is produced. It is true that each school is apt to run to a particular set of words, and a master like Tennyson or Browning sometimes introduces a number of new words and phrases which speedily become the literary fashion. Writers of power are still more likely to rescue from oblivion some stray archaisms. But the literary language is the standard, and is held by conservative influences much more than it is disturbed by innovating forces. The laws of literary art are always the same, though the ideas which literature must present are progressive.

Dialects have a strange persistence when once

established. The very essence of a dialect is, however, that it differs from other dialects. Thus we have Yorkshire, Dorset, Norfolk, Scotch, and Irish, each with its own racy, antique flavor. Imperfect English, as spoken by Germans and Frenchmen, is not entitled to be regarded as a dialect, nor are we willing to recognize *technical* English as a variety, although the nomenclature of botany and chemistry is unintelligible to those who have not made a special study of it. Technical English is simply ordinary English applied to special subject-matter.

Colloquial English and dialectic English are full of what we call slang expressions, started by the whims of individuals. If these are needed or "fill a known want"—to use a slang expression—they are sometimes retained, and, after a time, admitted into the ordinary English and even into literary English when they have proved their value. This was the case with *mob* and *fun*, which are less than a century old, and doubtless will be the case with that very useful word, *crank*. To the philologist a word is interesting as a specimen, and slang, even low slang, may have a scientific value. Dialectic survivals, as in our New England speech, may illustrate a law or prove an ancient usage. It is not the dignity of a word that measures its worth as an illustration.

Returning to the consideration of the words

we have borrowed from the Celtic tongues, we must notice that most of them are of low origin and belong to colloquial or ordinary English. None of them express abstract ideas. The following were taken into old French from the Celtic, for French is not entirely of Latin origin, but contains some words taken from the Celtic tongues of old Gaul, and some from the Frankish, the language of the Teutonic conquerors of France. From the French some of these passed into English. The list is not a long one (about seventy words), and contains, among others, *billiards, brisket, car, carry, carpenter, quay, bobbin, cloak, baggage, gravel, varlet, valet, vassal, piece.* Some of these words are not found in modern French, as *brisket, cloak, carry,* which are obsolete in France, though *carrière,* for career, or the path along which one is carried to success or failure has been retained. Carpenter meant originally a maker of cars or wagons, and was taken into low Latin as *carpentarius,* a wood-worker, thence into French, thence into English after the Conquest. Baggage is cognate with our English *bag,* and illustrates the point before alluded to, that an old English word and a Celtic word may be much alike, since both are of Aryan origin. Baggage is undoubtedly French from Celtic. We should not have the well-known phrase "bag and baggage" were both words from the same tongue.

The words *basket, brag, bog, druid, cabin, flannel, bump, dagger, peak* (found also in French), *glen,* and some fifty others are of Celtic origin, but came into English at an early date.

The words *bard, brogue, brogan, clan, fun, collie, cosey, plaid, shamrock, banshee,* and *whiskey* are from the Celtic tongues of Ireland, Scotland, or Wales, but they are of comparatively recent appearance in English. Brogue means a stout, coarse shoe, but has taken up the meaning of dialectic pronunciation. Milton uses *clan,* and Goldsmith *fun.* Plaid is in *Johnson's Dictionary;* it is undoubtedly Gaelic, and is cognate with Latin *pellis* (a skin) and the English fell. Spenser uses the word shamrock, but introduces it as an Irish word. Sir Walter Scott is responsible for the introduction of a number of Scotch words. Of course many names of the great geographical divisions—lakes, rivers, mountains—are of Celtic origin, and so are many surnames. These will be noticed hereafter. The names of the indigenous weeds and flowers of England are sometimes Celtic, like *cockel.* Both of these points testify to the antiquity of the Celtic occupation.

The names of many of the simplest kitchen utensils and materials are of Celtic origin, as: *spider, pie, bucket, bung, curd, crock, crockery, griddle, gruel, mop, kettle, kale, mug, noggin, posset, pudding, slab*—in the sense of viscous, "make the gruel thick and slab"—*skillet, pan,** and many others of similar character.

The presence of this marked Celtic element in kitchen nomenclature suggests that Celtic captives were held as household slaves by the Saxon conquerors, and that these preserved and handed down a number of their native words in familiar daily use. This inference is strengthened by the fact that the name which the Saxons gave the English Britons—*Welsch*, or strangers—was the same word they used for slave, *weal* meaning male slave, and *wylen* meaning female slave.

Again, the slang of the lowest class in London, the vernacular of the Artful Dodger and Charley Bates in *Oliver Twist*, contains a number of peculiar expressions, some of which are no doubt of ancient Celtic origin. Thus, in that argot a magistrate is a " beak," from the Celtic *beach;* "twig" is from *tuig*, to understand; "cove" from *coove*, a courteous person; " hook it " is from *thugad*, begone; "masher," from *meas*, elegant; "brick," from *brigh*, a courageous person; "cut your stick," from *cuit as teach*, leave the house. To "kick the bucket," to "make your lucky," and to "cheese it"† have,very likely, origins of the same

---

* *Pan*, though taken into English from the Welsh, may have been taken by the Welsh from the Latin *patina*.

† Query : Why is a constable called a *cop* in the same slang ? It can hardly be because he serves a *capias*.

character — that is, they may be Celtic phrases assimilated in pronunciation to English words with which they have no connection in meaning. "Cheese it" is conjectured to be from French *cesser* (to cease), which seems an unlikely source for a slang phrase, as "cease" is a dignified, bookish sort of a word to fall so low. "Cheese," in the expression "that's the cheese," is probably Gypsy, from the word meaning "thing" in the Romany dialect.

The presence of this singular element in low London slang affords at least a presumption that when the Saxons took possession of London,* then an important Celtic city, a certain number of Celts of the lowest class were unable to remove, and so perpetuated a few remnants of their language in the lowest stratum of society. However, it must be admitted that this lowest class of thieves and beggars in the cities of the Middle Ages was of such an anomalous character that it is dangerous to draw any inferences from such fragments of its speech as may have come down to us. Again, slang is so lawless in its changes, and is so rarely recorded, that slang dictionaries are full of conjectures. All of the above derivations

---

* The theory that London was entirely abandoned by the Celts is hardly tenable; but even if it were, the Saxons in occupying the deserted city would bring Celtic slaves with them.

are disputed. Still, there seems to be enough of the Celtic element to support the presumption, though perhaps not very strongly.

Other English words of probable Celtic origin are *babe, bad, bald, bludgeon, boast, clock, coax, cob, crag, crease, drudge, gown, hassock, lad, lass, racket,* (a noise—a tennis racket is Arabic), *flimsy*. For a full list *Skeat's Etymological Dictionary*, p. 757, may be consulted. The list is not very long, nor does it embrace many important words. For some reason Celts never hold their mother-tongue as tenaciously as do Teutons. Both Welsh and Irish seem likely to become extinct as spoken languages in the next century. The Celtic blood is widely diffused, and contributes valuable elements to the English character, but our linguistic debt to the race is slight. It is painful to reflect that these ancient tongues, representing the speech of one of the oldest branches of the Aryan stock, must disappear and leave no modern representatives; but such seems to be their destiny.

For a thorough modern examination of this question see *Skeat's English Etymology*, chap. xxii.

CHAPTER VI.

CLASSES OF LATIN DERIVATIVES.

WE will now take up the Latin and Romance element in our vocabulary. This is very much the most important element, constituting as it does over one-half of our dictionary words and a large proportion of those in actual use. It is as early an element as the Celtic, for Saxon took up some Latin words even before the invasion of Britain. A large number of Romance words came into the language from the French, and a few from Italian, Spanish, and Portuguese. Later the theological dissensions of the seventeenth century brought about the introduction of a good many Latin words directly from the Latin tongue. By far the greater number came from the French or Norman-French during the twelfth and thirteenth centuries, the formative period of the language, and contributed largely to the character of the new tongue. Sometimes the same Latin word was adopted into English twice, and took two meanings, classic and romantic. Thus, *pine* and

CLASSES OF LATIN DERIVATIVES. 57

punish are both from the Latin *pœna*, the latter through the French *punir*, being by two or three hundred years the younger English word. Compare also *chalice* and *calix*, *cadence* and *chance*, *regal* and *royal*.

Again, there are in our language words that have, to quote Professor Meiklejohn, "made their appearances—once through Latin, once through Norman-French, and once through ordinary French." These seem to live quietly side by side in our language, and no one asks by what claim they are here. They are useful; that is enough. Examples of such triplets are *legal*, *loyal*, and *leal*—leal used in Scotland, where it has a settled abode in the phrase "the land of the leal" —*fidelity*, *faithfulness*, and *fealty*. Faithfulness has two English suffixes on a Latin word.

The Latin words in our language have been classified in various ways, the common method being by dates and periods. Of the classifications by periods that given by Professor Meiklejohn is perhaps as satisfactory as any other. He makes four periods.

LATIN OF THE FIRST PERIOD.—This covers Latin words left in Britain by the Romans, and strictly numbers but six words: *castra*, *strata*, *colonia*, *fossa*, *portus*, and *vallum*. These words appear only in geographical names. The word *castra* has been colored by the usage of the locality where it was applied. Thus, in the north it is sounded hard, as in Lancaster, Doncaster, Tadcaster. In the Midland counties it takes the softer form, *cester*, as in Leicester, Towcester, and in the extreme west and south it takes the still softer form of *chester*, as in Chester, Manchester, Winchester, and others. The first syllable in these words is the Celtic name of the locality or river by which the camp was distinguished. *Strata* has also taken different forms in different parts of England, but has always been a prefix. One of the first things the Romans did was to drive a strongly-built military road from Richborough, near Dover, northward to the River Dee, where they formed a permanent camp, *Castra Stativa*, which is still called Chester. This road was called the "street," and by the Saxons "Watling Street." The word *strata*, in the forms of *strat*, *strad*, *stret*, and *streat*, is a part of the modern names of many towns, all of which are on this or some other great Roman road. Thus, we have Stratford-on-Avon, Stratton, Stradbroke, Stretton, Stretford, and Streatham, the other syllables in these cases being Saxon. *Colonia* we find in Colne, Lincoln, and others; *fossa* in Fossway, Fossbrooke, and Fossbridge; *portus* in Portsmouth and Bridgeport, and *vallum* in the words *wall*, *bailey* and *bailiff*. The Normans called the two courts in front of their castles the inner

CLASSES OF LATIN DERIVATIVES. 59

and outer *baileys*, and the officer in charge of them, the *bailiff*.* *Mile, pine, pose, port, wick* (a village), and *wine* probably entered the English language before A.D. 500, and therefore belong to this class in one sense.

LATIN ELEMENT OF THE SECOND PERIOD.—In the year 596 Pope Gregory the Great sent over to Kent a missionary called Augustine with forty monks. They were received by the King of Kent, allowed to settle in Canterbury, and to build a small cathedral there. This mission and the churches that grew out of it brought into old English a number of words from the Latin, most of which have survived in a different form. Among them are: *postol*, from *apostolus* (a person sent) ; *biscop*, from *episcopus* (an overseer); *calc*, from *calix* (a cup); *clerc*, from *clericus* (an ordained member of the Church) ; *munic*, from *monachus* (a solitary person); *preost*, from *presbyter* (an elder) ; *aelmesse*, from *eleemosune* (alms) ;† *regol*, from *regula* (a rule). To this period also belongs the in-

---

* There is some question about *bail*, *bailiff*, and *bailwick*. It is not certain that they are derived from *vallum* (an enclosing wall). The root is obscure, though certainly Latin, but possibly later than the first period, and through the Norman-French law-jargon.

† *Apostle, bishop, clerk, monk, priest,* and *alms* come to us really from Greek words, but through the Latin. We may note, too, that *presbyter* is not "priest writ large," as Milton said, but *priest* is *presbyter* writ small.

troduction of the words *butter, cheese, fig, cedar, pear, peach, lettuce, lily, pepper, pease, camel, lion, elephant, oyster, trout, pound, ounce, candle, table, marble.* We cannot be certain, however, that some of these words were not introduced into Anglo-Saxon before the migration from the Continent, since we have no complete glossary of all the dialects spoken by the invaders.

There is one word of this or an earlier period that is probably of Greek origin, and that is *church.* It seems to have been introduced very early into all the Teutonic tongues. The explanation usually given for the appearance of this word at so early a date is, that Ulphilas, a missionary from Constantinople, translated the Gospels for the use of the Moesian Goths, among whom he labored in the fourth century, and finding no equivalent for *church* in their language, transferred the word from the Greek, and so introduced it was taken up by the other Teutonic tribes. This is probably the true reason for its adoption, unless the Goths and other Teutons, who were allies of the Roman Empire and served in its legions, had already used the Greek name for a building with which they must have been familiar, and so Ulphilas found the word ready for his purpose.

LATIN OF THE THIRD PERIOD. — This is in reality French of the variety generally called Norman-French, which has its own peculiarities both in spelling and pronunciation. At the period of the Norman Conquest Parisian French did not hold its present position of literary supremacy. French grew out of the spoken dialects of Latin, and the Norman-French, when it came to be written, spelled *peuple, people; loyal, leal; royaume, realm; royal, real*, and so on. The Norsemen, to whom the valley of the Seine was ceded in 912, were, of course, originally Teutons, but when they settled in France they learned in course of time to speak French of the kind called Norman-French. This language was used in the English Court before the Norman Conquest, under Edward the Confessor, who came to the throne in 1042. He had been educated at the Norman Court, and insisted that the nobles about him should speak French.

William, Duke of Normandy, conquered England pretty thoroughly, and as he was a great administrator, covered the country with the feudal executive machinery. Thus, Norman-French became the language of the governmental and ecclesiastical world, of the universities, and, conjointly with Latin, of literature. The people held fast to their own tongue, nor did it cease entirely to be written, but it had no central standard, and of course began to change rapidly. A series of important political events, culminating with the loss of Normandy in 1204, detached England from France, drew all the people of England into a national organization, and aroused a national sentiment. The fact that the two languages were both spoken in England for so many years, one by the upper class and the other by the body of the people, would naturally result in the vernacular English taking a number of words from the courtly Norman. In 1272 Robert of Gloucester wrote a metrical chronicle in English and used a large number of French words. All others writers of the transition period, Robert of Brun, Layamon, etc., use French words in varying proportions, though Layamon (1155) is almost purely Saxon in his vocabulary. The triumph of English may be said to be marked by an Act of Parliament, passed in 1362 under Edward III., by which it was enacted that English should be used in the Law Courts. Previous to this the statement or pleadings had been made in English, but the judgment entered in Latin. Chaucer was born about 1340 and died in 1400, and his admirable poems, written in English, contain about the same proportion of words of French derivation as is used by a modern writer, and mark the firm establishment of a new language, a language of composite vocabulary but of Teutonic structure. The English accepted no French idioms, or at least very few, though they took up many thousand French words. Consequently, we are to-day at liberty to use as many Latin words as we like, but few Latin constructions, if we wish to speak or write English.

The words brought into the language by the Normans are nearly all those connected in any way with the governing or more important social class. Nearly all the vocabulary of knight-errantry and feudalism is of French origin. Such words are *arms, armor, assault, joust, lance, shield, greaves, page, mistress, homage, fealty, esquire, herald.* *Vassal* comes from *vassus*, a Celtic word meaning man, introduced into French. The same word gave us also *varlet* and *valet.* *Scutcheon* meant originally *shield, scutum.* Then it came to mean heraldic devices painted on the shield. The word is used by carpenters in the original sense of a shield, to designate the plate of metal surrounding the key-hole and shielding the wood from injury. The terms connected with *archery*— that is, the radical terms, *bow, arrows, bolt, bowstring,* etc.—are Saxon, though the Normans added some technical terms referring to the ornamental details of the art.

This fact shows that the Saxons were archers before the Conquest, or rather bowmen, since *archer* is the Norman word from *arc*, a *bow*, and *bowman* is pure English. The practice of archery was, however, greatly improved under Norman rule.

All the words connected with hunting as a sport are Norman, and so are the names of many of the game-birds and animals. But a *deer*, a *hart*, and a *stag* remained Saxon, the word *cerf* never taking root in England. The Saxons were too familiar with the deer to give up the name, but the word *venison*, from *venari* (to hunt), is French. *Quarry*, as a place from which to take stones for building, is French—the Normans were great architects; but *quarry*, a hunting term, is from another source, the French *quer* from *cor* (the heart), which was given to the dogs. *Quarry*, in the other signification, is from *quadrare* (to square).

Nearly all the French words of these classes have been relegated to poetry, or have become antiquated by the change of methods of war and hunting. *Arm, shield, standard, forest*, are words in common use, but some hundreds of others of this class are either entirely obsolete or are to be found only in the list of literary or poetical words. To many of them a tinge of affectation attaches. Under no circumstances can we now call a horse a *courser* or *charger*, though, for that matter, the radical English word *steed*, applied to *stud*, is equally obsolete. *Brace*, as applied to a couple of birds, has held its place very well. It is derived from the old French *brace* (an arm), from which the derived meanings of sustaining or bracing up and encircling in the arms, or embracing, flow naturally. The meaning of brace, or couple, possibly comes from the fact that we have two arms, possibly because a pair of birds were tied together with a string. In the same way *leash* (a thong to hold dogs) got the signification of three, since three dogs were usually tied together.*

The old romances ascribe the invention of the vocabulary of the chase to Sir Tristram, and the *Morte d'Arthur* says:

"Mesemeth alle gentylmen that beren old armes oughte of ryght to honour Syre Tristram for the godly termes that gentylmen have and use, and shall to the day of dome, that thereby in a manner all men maye discover a gentylman fro a yoman, and from a yoman a vylane. For he that gentyl is wylle drawe hym unto gentyl tatches, and to followe the customes of noble gentylmen."

The *Book of St. Albans*, first printed in 1486, is very full on the subject of the technical terms of the chase. These are nearly all Norman words. This precision in the use of terms relating to hunting is still characteristic of Englishmen,

---

* *Leash* once meant a brace and a half (see Shak., King Henry IV. Part I., Act II., Scene iv., line 7): "Sirrah, I am sworn brother to a leash of drawers, and can call them all by their Christian names, as — Tom, Dick, and Francis." Now it has gone back to the original meaning of the thong, and usually binds *two* dogs together, not *three*.

though so many of the old words have become obsolete. The Normans carried this affectation to an excess. Thus, Dame Juliana Berners, the reputed author of the *Book of St. Albans*, tells us that in gentle speech it is said that "the hawk *jouketh*, not sleepeth ; she *refourmeth* her feders, and not picketh her feders ; she *rowsith*, and not shaketh herselfe ; she *mantellyth*, and not stretchyth, when she putteth her legges from her one after another, and her wynges follow her legges ; and when she hath mantylled her and bryngeth both her wynges togyder over her backe, ye shall say your hawkye *warbelleth* her wynges." Further, we are told we must not use names of multitudes promiscuously, but we are to say a "*congregacion* of people," a "*hoost* of men," a "*felyshyppinge* of yomen," and a "*bevy* of ladyes ;" we must speak of a ." *herde* of dere," " swannys," " crannys," or "wrenys," a "*sege* of nyghtingales," a "*flyghte* of doves," a "*claterynge* of choughes," a "*pryde* of lyons," a "*sleuthe* of beeres," a "*gagle* of geys," a "*skulke* of foxes," a "*sculle* of frerys," a "*pontificality* of prestys," and a "*superfluyte* of nonnes ;" and so of other human and brute assemblages. In like manner, in dividing game for the table, the animals were not carved, but a "dere was *broken*, a goose *reryd*, a chekyn *frusshed*, a coney *unlaced*, a crane *dysplayed*, a curlew *unjoynted*, a qualle *wyngged*, a lamb *sholdered*, a heron *dys-*

membered, a peacock *dysfygured*," etc. A strict observance of all these niceties of speech was more important as an indication of good breeding, or, in the words of Dame Juliana Berners, as a "means of dystynguishing gentylmen from ungentylmen," than was a rigorous conformity to the rules of grammar or even to those of the moral law; nor would it be difficult to find even now people who judge others by a similar linguistic standard. The slang of "society" seems to be as old and as artificial as society itself.

CHAPTER VII.

ARTIFICIAL CHARACTER OF THE LATIN ELEMENT.

It will be noticed that a large proportion of the artificially-used words mentioned in the last chapter are Norman-French. Even now if we set ourselves to work in cold blood to force words into unnatural uses we draw our material from the same class. Most of the fanciful expressions which the affected and self-conscious literary fashion called Euphuism brought into use, come from the Latin side of our language. It is difficult to be affected in any Teutonic tongue unless, indeed, we affect a plain, unfinished rusticity. As we shall see later, a large number of French derivatives have become thoroughly anglicized, but to many others a slight flavor of affectation still attaches. We may notice, too, in passing, that a certain set of artificial expressions is still the shibboleth of fashionable society, just as it was in the time of Dame Juliana Berners. These are generally manufactured in London, but the vocabulary is so limited as greatly to restrict conversation among those who use it. The society vocabulary of the fifteenth century seems to have been much less meagre than is that of the last quarter of the nineteenth.

A great body of Norman-French words which have been permanently adopted are those appertaining to the legal and ecclesiastical professions and to philosophical conceptions. These classes of words, especially the second and third, frequently come direct from the Latin, which remained till the eighteenth century the language of scholars and theologians all over the Christian world. Milton wrote his controversial tracts in Latin. We will revert to these words under the head of words of the trades and professions. Nearly all titles of nobility, and of the sacred orders, of Masonry, etc., are Latin of this period. Indeed, the Normans gave us the words *title, dignity, noble* (from *nosco, nobilis, known*), etc.; also the specific titles *duke (dux), marquis, count (comes), peer (par), marshall*, etc. *Marquis* is the officer in charge of the *mark* or *border*, and is therefore originally a Teutonic word embedded in French. *Marshal* is of the same class. *Mereschall* meant originally in Frankish the man who had charge of the horses, and has retained in the French word *maréchal* (blacksmith or farrier) another branch of its original meaning. But on another side it developed to mean in French the leading military officer, as "*Le Maréchal Ney.*" With us this second meaning has been arrested, and denotes only one who has charge of a procession, or the executive federal court officer. Our word *martial*, from Mars, the god of war, is from a totally different root, and came to us along with *jovial, saturnine, mercurial*, and a number of other words and expressions from the ancient pseudo-science of astrology. Those who were born when certain planets were in the "ascendant" were supposed to partake of certain "influences." As, however, the Latin contained the adjective *martialis*, it is not absolutely certain that the word martial comes to us through the astrological term.

There is a well-worn but still interesting quotation from *Ivanhoe* which illustrates the relative positions of certain Norman and English words, and, indirectly, the relations of the two peoples :

"'. . . I advise thee to call off Fangs and leave the herd to their destiny, which, whether they meet with bands of travelling soldiers, or of outlaws, or of wandering pilgrims, can be little else than to be converted into Normans before morning, to thy no small ease and comfort.'

"'The swine turned into Normans to my comfort!' quoth Gurth. 'Expound that to me, Wamba, for my brain is too dull and my mind too vexed to read riddles.'*

"'Why, how call you these grunting brutes running about on their four legs?' demanded Wamba.

"'Swine, fool, swine,' said the herd; 'every fool knows that.'

"'And *swine* is good Saxon,' said the jester; 'but how call you the sow when she is flayed, and drawn, and quartered, and hung by the heels like a traitor?'

"'Pork,' answered the swineherd.

"'I am glad every fool knows that too,' said Wamba; 'and *pork*, I think, is good Norman-French, and so when the brute lives and is in the charge of a Saxon slave, she goes by her Saxon name; but becomes a Norman and is called *pork* when she is carried to the castle-hall to feast among the nobles. What dost thou think of that, friend Gurth, ha?'

"'It is but too true doctrine, friend Wamba, however it got into thy fool's pate.'

"'Nay, I can tell you more,' said Wamba, in the same tone. 'There is old Alderman Ox continues to hold his Saxon epithet while he is under the charge of serfs and bondsmen such as thou;

---

* *Read* and *riddles* are from the same root, meaning "to interpret." *Riddles* (something to be explained) was not plural. It has, however, lost the final *s*. *Riddle* (a large seine) is from another Saxon word.

but becomes Beef, a fiery French gallant, when he arrives before the worshipful jaws that are to consume him. Mynherr Calf, too, becomes *Monsieur de Veau* in the like manner; he is Saxon when he requires tendance, and takes a Norman name when he becomes a matter of enjoyment.'"

From the Norman-French came a number of general or class names, while the corresponding specific names for individual things are mostly Saxon. *Animal* and *beast* are French, but *dog, cat, weasel, fox, bee, horse, mare, sheep,* etc., are Saxon. Again, if the Norman gave us *palace, castle, mansion,* we have kept the Saxon words *house, home,* and *cottage*. Against the French word *table* we have the humbler but more hospitable word *board*. *Dish*, though originally from the Latin *discus*, was naturalized so early as to come into the same class with *pitcher, mug, jug,* and *spoon*. We may conjecture that our Saxon ancestors ate with their knives, since *fork* is Latin; still they must have used forks, though not for the table, before the Conquest, since the word is found in Saxon and is from *furca*, not from *fourchette*.*
Mr. Spaulding observes: "We use a foreign term naturalized when we speak of color, but if we tell what that color is, as *red, yellow, black, green,* or

---

* We may make this conjecture with the more confidence, since we know that forks were not used in England for the table till the seventeenth century.

brown, we use an English word. We are Romans when we speak in a general way of moving, but we are Teutons if we *leap* or *spring*, or *slip* or *slide*, or *crawl*, or *fall*, or *walk*, or *run*, *swim*, *creep*, or *fly*. The more modern particularized colors which were not differentiated by our ancestors, like *mauve, scarlet, crimson, vermilion, carmine*, etc., come under a different head. Many of them are technical trade names, derived from dyes, like *carmine* and *crimson*, from *kermes, cochineal* from Spanish, through the Arabic."

The general effect of the Norman-French infusion of words was to give us a large number of synonyms, one of which is of Latin, the other of Teutonic extraction, like *flower* and *bloom, stream* and *river, language* and *speech, pitch* and *degree, wife* and *spouse, miserable* and *wretched*, etc. Each member of these pairs of words has a slightly different meaning, and goes properly with different modifying adjectives and fits different figurative usages. For instance, we can speak of a stream of talk or of ideas, but a river of either would be rather an unpleasant image. We say a *high pitch* and a *low pitch*, but not low degree, for this has a special meaning, and is an antiquated expression. Again, we say *mother-tongue* and *fine language*, but not mother-language nor fine tongue. *Language* and *tongue* are based on the same verbal metaphor, cause for effect, or instrument for product, since *language* is from *lingua*, tongue; but the two words have now entirely different shades of meaning, some of which are hardly distinguishable. *Language* has reference to the words themselves and to the grammatical construction, *tongue* to the pronunciation and to the specific language. " His tongue bewrayeth him." " He used the English tongue." " Bad language " has an idiomatic meaning of its own, equivalent not to a bad tongue, but to blasphemous words. *Speech* is almost equivalent to spoken language, and can hardly be applied to written words. It would be better to say " His book was written in the Latin language " instead of "in the Latin tongue." We feel that *tongue* is the more archaic and poetic word. English is full of these niceties which we learn by usage, and many of them grew out of the fact that our vocabulary is drawn from two great reservoirs, the stores in each of which have a slightly different character, corresponding to the national spirit of the people which originally used them. We are not aware of the great number of these idioms or peculiar usages ·of words until we read English written by a foreigner who has attempted to learn the language after maturity or through books.

Synonyms never cover exactly the same ground. Thus, some uses of *language* are equivalent to some uses of *tongue*, and other uses of *tongue* are exchangeable for some uses of *speech*. If we represent the notions or concepts covered by the word *language* as enclosed in a circle, then the circle which represents the word *tongue* would be rather smaller, and would intersect it. The space common to the two circles would represent those meanings common to the two words. If, now, we represent the meanings of the word *speech* by another circle, this must intersect both and also cover a portion of the space common to the two. It should be the smallest of the three. Only the metaphorical or secondary uses of *tongue* and *speech* are here considered. The primary meaning of *tongue* is the organ of speech and taste, and for our present purpose we may consider the primary meaning of *speech* to be vocal utterance. These meanings are excluded because we are considering the words as synonyms. The special meanings of *speech* are but few, like "human speech," which is really broader than "human language." In nearly all cases either the word *language* or the word *tongue* could be substituted for the word *speech*, though, of course, the reverse is not true. The distinctions and likenesses of the words may be represented by the circles on the next page.

No two words are exact synonyms, because even if the meanings are almost identical, the lit-

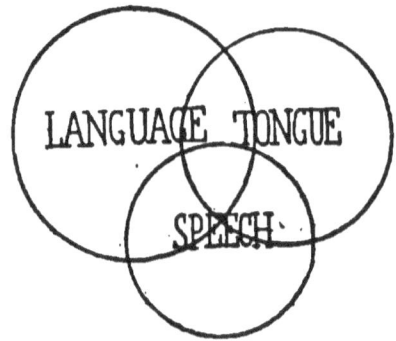

erary flavor is different. One of the words is always the right word for the place, though the difference is frequently so small that it is not worth while to consider it — at least in ordinary prose. "*De minimis non curat lex*"—and it were to "consider too curiously" to attempt to discriminate the significations of *begin* and *commence*, or *trustworthy* and *reliable;* but we should almost always use *begin* and *trustworthy* on account of their Saxon force. Nevertheless, there are cases where we should prefer to use the word *commence*. "Commenced operations," for instance, seems to imply preparation and design more than does began operations; but it is rather a colloquial expression at best. When two words substantially equivalent are in use, the genius of the language assigns them to different duties or drops one of them.

There are a number of expressions consisting of two words of the same meaning, one of which is English and the other Norman-French. These are survivals of the time when Norman words were sinking into the English language, and some persons understood a Norman term and others an English one. Mr. Earle gives a list of these double expressions, some of which are given below:

Act and deed.   Metes and bounds.
Aid and abet.   Will and testament.
Bag and baggage.   Use and wont.
Head and chief.   Pray and beseech.

The Prayer-book, revised 1542-1548, and founded largely on ancient usage, is apparently influenced by this feeling for a double vocabulary, and uses the expressions "acknowledge and confess," "assemble and meet together," "dissemble and cloak," "humble and lowly." Other instances of survivals of the same usage can be found in the writings of the sixteenth and seventeenth centuries.

This great gain of material to the vocabulary of the English language was accompanied by some loss, of the same nature as the gain, and by other losses of a more serious character. The net result, as seen summed up in the great Chaucer, was of course very great gain. In symplifying the grammar a number of fine terminations were lost. The *um* of the dative plural, the *en*, *an*, *era*, and *ena*, the *igenne* and *igendum* of the Saxons, could not have been other than dignified and sonorous sounds. We have the admirable syllable *ing* for the present participle, but the beautiful termination *ende* must have been less apt to degenerate into a nasal sound. The strong suffix *dom* which we have in *kingdom, wisdom, Christendom*, etc., might well have been retained in many other terminals. *Heritage* is a grand word, but it might have divided territory with the still stronger Saxon word *birthdom*. We might have appropriated *heritage* to our material, and *birthdom* to our spiritual inheritance. Of course, in symplifying the grammar and passing from an inflected to a synthetic language, the terminals must go, for that was the very essence of the change, and if we look regretfully on the loss of some words and sounds, we must try to keep unharmed every element we have of the old English tongue.

LATIN OF THE FOURTH PERIOD.—The Norman-French words entered the national language— that is, the tongue of the people; but in the sixteenth and seventeenth centuries the revival of learning and the increased interest in theological and philosophical discussion brought about by the Reformation resulted in the introduction into the written or literary language of a large number of words directly from Latin. Milton, and, later, Sir Thomas Browne, never hesitated to anglicize a Latin term, and, in consequence, many "long tailed words in *osity* and *ation*" crowded into the English language, most of them, happily, doomed to a speedy death and entombment in our large dictionaries. Thus, words like *exeruncate* — not a bad word, by the way — *septentrionality, moribundiousness*, strutted in the books of the learned for a brief day and then disappeared. Even Dr. Johnson would have called these "ink-horn terms," though they were used by good writers.

Words direct from the Latin can readily be distinguished from words from Latin through French. French nouns come from the accusatives of Latin nouns, the terminations being much disfigured. Frequently, as said before, we have received the word through both channels, that through the French being the more disguised from the fact that it was received into the oral language through the ear, while the Latin derivative was transplanted bodily to a written page. The following is an imperfect list of such duplicates:

FROM LATIN.

DIRECT.	THROUGH FRENCH.
Antecessor.	Ancestor.
Benediction.	Benison.
Cadence.	Chance.
Conception.	Conceit.
Consuetude.	{ Custom. { Costume.
Example.	Sample.
Fabric.	Forge.

DIRECT.	THROUGH FRENCH.
Faction.	Fashion.
Fact.	Feat.
Fragile.	Frail.
History.	Story.
Hospital.	Hotel.
Particle.	Parcel.
Pauper.	Poor.
Perseçute.	Pursue.
Pungent.	Poignant.
Quiet.	Coy.
Separate.	Sever.
Tradition.	Treason.
Zealous.	Jealous.
Captive.	Caitiff.
Radius.	Ray.

It will be observed that the words in the second column are, on the whole, shorter, and have more of the vernacular character than those in the first; and some of them, as, for example, *forge, poor, ray*, sound like Teutonic words, so firmly have they become imbedded in English speech, and so entirely have their characteristic Romance terminations disappeared. This, of course, results from the fact that they were spoken words, taken from a living language, and not book words, taken from the literature of a dead language, and were assimilated by the wear and tear of oral speech.

CHAPTER VIII.

LITERARY CHARACTER OF THE LATIN DERIVATIVES.

WE are frequently counselled to avoid the use of Latin derivatives, and are told that the quality of earnestness, simplicity, and power belongs to the English element of our tongue. This caution certainly can apply only to long words with Latin terminations. The following is an imperfect list of words of Latin root, of one syllable, which have been in our language since 1400, and, like the Huguenots in America, or the Normans in Ireland, have become more native than the natives themselves :

Add, air, art, beast, blame, blanch, boast, boil, cape, case, cause, cease, chance, change, charm, chaste, cheer, chief, clear, cook, cope, course, court, crime, crown, cure, damn, dance, doubt, dress, ease, face, faith, fail, false, fume, feast, fierce, fool, force, form, fount, gay, grace, grant, grieve, guide, guile, haste, haunt, host, hour, join, joy, judge, large, mass, meat, moist, name, nurse, pace, pain, paint, pair, pale, pass, peace, plain, please, point, pomp, poor, pope, port, pound, pray, preach, prude, pounce, prince, prize, prove, pure, purge, quaint, quit, rent, robe, rose, rote, route, rude, saint, sauce, save, school, serve, siege, sign, sir, sort, space, spend, spouse, squire, strait, taste, tent, term, turn, vain, vice.

Here are more than one hundred monosyllables of Latin lineage in constant use since Chaucer's time, and the number of dissyllables of similar character is much greater. There is no reason that we should avoid these words, and it would be harmful to try to do so. But Latin sentence-movement must be avoided at all hazards, and the long Latin derivatives must be handled with skill and discretion. In the use of words we should be independent, but with Saxon proclivities.

Professor Earle says that "A Norman family settled in England and edited the English language," which is rather a neat epigram; but would it not be nearer the truth to say that the English people edited their own language and Chaucer published it? The language grew out of the usage of the people who were relieved from any literary supervision for nearly three hundred years, and it still grows very slowly, in spite of literary supervision and criticism.

One influence which tended to retain archaisms

arose from the successive translations of the Bible. Wycliffe, in the fourteenth century, translated it into middle English. The subsequent revisers, Tyndall (1526), Coverdale (1580), and the revisers in King James' reign, were each familiar with the Bible used before their day, and each version was founded on its predecessor. Each reviser was desirous to retain archaisms that had become associated with the text, and at the same time to make the book "understanded of the people." Thus there was a sort of transmission in a written book and in the minds of the people of phrases and words which might otherwise have dropped out of remembrance. The Bible has undoubtedly been a conservative influence for the English element of our composite language. Its relations to English speech and thought have been very close, and it is and has been the storehouse of religious phraseology. Professor Marsh says : " Wycliffe must be considered as having originated the diction which for five centuries has constituted the consecrated dialect of the English speech, and Tyndall as having given to it that finish and perfection which have so admirably adapted it to the expression of religious doctrine and sentiment, and to the narrative of the remarkable series of historical facts which are recorded in the Christian Scriptures."

Professor Marsh calls attention to the fact that the Norman words added greatly to our stock of rhymes. He says: "Many of the French words which first appear in Chaucer were introduced for the sake of the rhyme, and not infrequently taken as they stood in the poems which he translated or paraphrased, and there is almost as great a preponderance of French rhymes in his own original works." "The Squire's Tale" has not been traced to any foreign source, and is believed to be of Chaucer's own invention; but of the six hundred and twenty-two lines of which that fragment consists, one hundred and eighty-seven end with Romance words, though the proportion of Anglo-Saxon words in the poem is more than ninety per cent. Puttenham, late in the sixteenth century, is severe upon Gower for helping himself to French rhymes when English would not serve his turn. He says: "For a licentious maker is in truth but a bungler, not a Poet. Such men were in effect the most part of all your old rimers, and specially Gower, who to make up his rime would for the most part write his terminal syllable with false orthographie, and menie times not stickle to put in a plaine French word for an English; and so by your leave do many of our common rimers at this day."

Chaucer concludes the complaint of Mars with this lamentation:

"And eke to me it is a great penaunce,
Sith rhyme in English hath such scarcite,
To follow word by word the curiosite
Of Graunson, flour of them that make in Fraunce."

Professor Marsh points out also that double rhymes are very frequently made by French words. Double rhymes are words which have the same terminal unaccented, and a rhyming accented penult — like "duty," "beauty;" "ringing," "singing;" "gladness," sadness." Many of the rhyming couplets among the English derivatives of our language are heavy monosyllables, and the double rhyming couplets from the same class are inflected words, like "chiming," "rhyming," or the antiquated forms in *eth* and *est;* "lyeth," "trieth;" "lovest," "provest," which last are awkward enough. We become rather tired of the double rhymes in *ing*, and double rhymes made of an unaccented word preceded by a rhyming word have an element of the ridiculous, like "write it" and "smite it." Therefore, as double rhymes are very pleasing to the ear, and as we have but few graceful and effective polysyllabic endings of Saxon etymology, versifiers will generally be forced to seek them in the Roman and Romance elements of our speech, and thus "the frequency of double rhymes tends to increase the proportion of Latin words in our poetic dialect." This is unfortunate, to say the least, for any artificial pressure on our language must be regarded as likely to be injurious; and Professor Marsh goes on to say that our poetic diction might render a great service to the language if it could revive some of the Saxon inflectional terminals employed so charmingly by Chaucer, as, for instance:

> "With hearty will they sworen and *assenten*,
> To all this thing ther said not o wight nay;
> Beseeching him of grace or that they *wenten*,
> That he would granten hem a certain day."

"Mrs. Browning's fine poem, the 'Cry of the Children,' contains one hundred and sixty verses, with alternate double and single rhymes, and of course there are forty pairs of double rhymes, or eighty double-rhymed words. The proportion of Romance words in the whole poem is but eight per cent., but of the double-rhymed terminals thirty per cent. are Romance, so that nearly one-fourth of the Romance words introduced into the poem are found in the double rhymes, while of the eighty single-rhymed terminals seventy are certainly Saxon, and of the remaining ten, three or four are probably so."

Tennyson and Browning revived a number of archaic words — most of them for the sake of their associations—which have permanently enriched poetic diction and through this the literary language. Poetry is one root of linguistic growth, and the words it introduces to good society or

CHARACTER OF LATIN DERIVATIVES. 87

rescues from oblivion, though not numerous, not infrequently obtain or resume good standing, and are sometimes of great value.

In general, the Romance element of our language lends itself to special subjects of which the nomenclature is Romance, and to all abstract as opposed to concrete treatment of a subject. Its literary value is quite equal to that of the Saxon element, but if wrongly used it can harm literary expression, whereas Saxon can never work harm even if used to excess. It is the Latin of the Fourth Period which is apt to give a scholastic and ponderous effect, not the Romance element, for that has become a part of our mother-tongue. The monosyllables mentioned on page 81 are idiomatic, and dissyllables like *defeat, delay, gentle, story, severe, fortune, honest, humble, intent, pity, prayer, promise, study, tyrant, usage, easy, monster*, and hundreds of others have been used so long — they all occur in Chaucer — that they have acquired the colloquial quality as fully as any Saxon derivatives that could be named. How could we do without the words *people, party, perfect, office, repent, report*, etc., all so firmly imbedded in English speech that they come to our lips when needed as readily as any Saxon synonyms would, if indeed there be Saxon synonyms for them all. The particles and little connecting words, the pronouns, prepositions, and auxilliary verbs of our language are from the Saxon side. We cannot dispense with them, but if any color is to be given to style, the Latin as well as the Romance element in our tongue must be used. Furthermore, if sonorousness is to be attained (a quality usually to be eliminated, but not always,) we must use the long Latin words in their proper places. They give the basis—the heavy resonance—the carrying power—needed occasionally, though rarely. But they should be used instinctively, not of malice aforethought, and so indeed must all words. A man might as well insist on expending his paternal inheritance to the exclusion of what he had received from his mother, as to insist on using Saxon words only.

Examination will prove that many striking images in our literature derive their force from Latin and Romance words. Matthew Arnold calls Shelley " a *pale, uneffectual angel, beating* his *luminous* wings in the *void.*" None of these words can be changed, because there are associations with nearly all of them. A "wan, weak ghost, flapping his bright wings in the emptiness," or any other Saxon paraphrase, is trash. *Pale* and *uneffectual* are connected in a well-known quotation. *Beating*, applied to wings, is used by Rosetti in another beautiful passage, and had been applied to the Angel of Death by John Bright in an oratorical passage of rare elevation and purity. *Luminous* has scientific associations as a source of light. *Void* suggests cosmic space through which a divine message might be striving in vain to approach us. So all these words strengthen each other.*

When Shakspeare's characters are to make a plain, strong statement (as is pointed out by Professor Corsen), they frequently use Saxon monosyllables; but when their emotional and intellectual natures are wrought up to a stress of passion, and they have time to express their feelings, they avail themselves of the stores of picturesque and sonorous words which come from Latin and French. Thus Macbeth, speaking of the blood on his hands, says that it would

"the *multitudinous* seas *incarnadine;*"

but he has worked up to that tremendous, polysyllabic, exaggerated expression of guilt through simpler Saxon words. When he hears that his wife is dead, he falls back in his chair with a groan, and says:

"She should have died hereafter:
There would have been a time for such a word.
To-morrow, and to-morrow, and to-morrow,
Creeps in its petty pace from day to day,
To the *last syllable* of *recorded time.*"

* Examine Shelley's "Adonais" and the "Sensitive Plant," and note that the elevated images are usually presented in Latin and Romance words.

The image called up by the two Romance words *syllable* and *recorded* is the most sublime in literature. No other words would be so powerful. No other words would have brought before us the image of the Angel of Eternity announcing the close of time, as it arose in the mind of the transgressor of the moral law.

But when Macbeth is giving an order or describing something he sees—though it be an illusion—his language is Saxon:

"Go, bid thy *mistress*, when my drink is ready
She strike upon the bell. Get thee to bed!
Is this a dagger, which I see before me,
The handle toward my hand? Come, let me clutch thee:
I have thee not, and yet I see thee still."

Antony says of Cleopatra:

"Age cannot wither her, or *custom* stale
Her *infinite variety*."

One of the most intellectually satisfying images in the "Sonnets" lies in two Saxon words, but the thing imaged is introduced by Romance words. Lamenting the degrading and narrowing effect of his vocation as a purveyor of public amusement, Shakspeare says:

"Thence comes it that my name *receives* a brand
And almost thence my *nature* is *subdued*
To what it works in, like the dyer's hand."

Many of the great phrases in the "Collects" exemplify the dual nature of English. For instance, " Pour upon them the *continual** dew of thy blessing." The Romance word has the same quality of inevitableness as the Saxon ones, *dew* and *blessing*. Both come from the heart of the language. It is unnecessary to multiply examples.

We may say in conclusion that English is a composite language; that each element has its own value; that to try to limit ourselves to Saxon results in baldness and sterility—the danger of our age; that to overwork the Latin results in inflation and pomposity, and that to translate adequate Saxon expressions into Latin equivalents, as is sometimes done, under the impression that we must use a more elevated diction, is in such bad taste that no one who reads needs be warned against it. Nothing but careful reading of good literature and constant practice will give us that feeling for words which will enable us—supposing, in the first place, that we have something to say— to use the two elements of our vocabulary so as to get the value of each.

Still, the examination of etymologies will be found to be of considerable benefit in increasing our power of appreciating verbal refinements. It

---

* A rule of modern rhetoric would change *continual* to *continuous*, thereby spoiling the phrase.

is true that many of those who have used words with the greatest delicacy and originality have not even known that the English language was compounded of two elements. But in many of our writers, whose claim to be considered literary artists is undisputed, as De Quincey, Lamb, Lowell, Thackeray—to go no further—it is evident that the knowledge of classical etymology has added to their command of words and their power of using them in new relations, and of bringing out novel and striking shades of meaning.

In reference to the number of words in our language, and the number derived from each great source, Max Müller says: *"Skeat's Etymological Dictionary of the English Language*, which confines itself to primary words—that is to say, which would explain *luck*, but not *lucky*, *unlucky*, or *luckless; multitude*, but not *multitudinous*, etc.—deals with no more than 13,500 entries. Of these, 4000 are of Teutonic origin, 5000 are taken from the French, 2700 direct from Latin, 250 from Celtic, and the rest (1250) from various sources. A language is, after all, not so bewildering a thing as it seems to be, when we hear of a dictionary of 250,000 words. For all the ordinary purposes of life a dictionary of 4000 words would be quite sufficient."

The material of the English language may therefore be taken to be about 13,500 words. The number of entries in our great dictionaries is swelled by including all possible compounds, multitudes of technical scientific words, and all the parts of speech except plurals and possessives, giving, for instance, under *love, loveless, lovely, lovingly, unlovely*, etc., and by including obsolete words and spellings, and many temporary and slang words manufactured for some special use. To put the vocabulary of educated persons at 4000 words only, would, however, seem rather illiberal, although the vocabulary of agricultural laborers in England is said not to exceed 600 words.

There are a few hybrid words in the language made by giving a Saxon termination to a Latin stem, or by compounding elements of any two languages into a single word. Some of these are: *interloper* (Latin-Dutch), *keelhaul* (Dutch-Scandinavian), *tarpaulin* (Latin-English), *chapman, Christmas, partake, pastime, saltpetre, bankrupt*, and many others of the same double nature. The Latin prefix *dis* and the English prefix *mis** are joined freely to verbs of either root. *Out* and *over*—English prefixes—can be compounded with

---

* *Mis* is, however, also a French prefix, from Latin *minus* —as in *mischief, miscreant, misalliance*. But *mis* as in *misdeed*, is English and connected with *miss*, and has a slightly different force. *Miscarry, misapply, misdirect*, are hybrid words.

words from all sources. The termination *ness*—
pure English—is given to as many Latin words as
English, and so is the prefix *fore;* but in these
cases we should rank the word for literary classification according to the character of its principal
parts. *Disburden* and *disbelieve*, for instance, have
the same Saxon flavor that *burden* and *believe*
have. The same is true of such words as *forecastle*, *forejudge*, *forefront*. They remain French
in spite of their Saxon prefix.

We will close the examination of the character
of the Latin element in English by an extract
from that delicate artist in words, Emerson. He
says ("English Traits"):

"The Saxon materialism and narrowness ex-
alted into the sphere of intellect makes the very
genius of Shakspeare and Milton. When it
reaches the pure element it treads the clouds as
securely as the adamant. Even in its elevations
materialistic, its poetry is common-sense inspired,
or iron raised to a white heat.

"The marriage of the two qualities is in their
speech. It is a tacit rule of the language to make
the frame and skeleton of Saxon words, and when
elevation or ornament is sought, to interweave the
Roman, but sparingly. Nor is a sentence made of
Roman words alone without loss of strength.
The children and laborers use Saxon unmixed.
The Latin unmixed is abandoned to the colleges

and Parliament. Mixture is a secret of the English island, and in their dialect the male principle is the Saxon, the female the Latin, and they are combined in every discourse. A good writer, if he has indulged in a Roman roundness, makes haste to chasten and nerve his period by English monosyllables."

CHAPTER IX.

MINOR SOURCES OF ENGLISH WORDS.

JUDGING from the relative numbers in the two great word-groups, the one from Teutonic, the other from Latin or Romance sources, we should conclude that English was a composite language. But it is not so except in its vocabulary. It is a language just as the United States is a nation—the evolution of a definite form of social consciousness. It is a Low-Germanic tongue, colored and enriched by an infusion of Italic derivatives. On examining the two groups we find that the Teutonic group contains: first, the words we most frequently use in everyday matters; second, the little words we use over and over again. Therefore, though we cannot think discursively on any subject without using words from both sources, we select a word from the Teutonic half of our store at least seven or eight times as often as we do one from the Latin-Romance half. Furthermore, the structure of the language is Teutonic, and the most impor-

MINOR SOURCES OF ENGLISH WORDS. 97

tant prefixes and suffixes are Teutonic. *Be* in *bemoan* and *befriend, for* in *forbid, mis* in *misdeed*, and the separable prefixes *after, in, off, on, out, over, under, up,* are old English. So, too, are the strong suffixes *ard*—seen in *coward, drunkard*, etc.—*dom, er, hood, ness, ship, sted, fast, fold, ful, ish,* and *ward*. Compare these to the Latin prefixes we use, like *non, extra, inter, post, pro, super, sub, trans, ultra,* and to the Latin suffixes like *age*—as in *courage, beverage,* etc.—*ancy, ate, ion, tion, ment, able, osity, ory, ation,* and the superior power and native character of the old English syllables are evident. As a rule, they strike us as growing more naturally out of the root. The Greek suffixes and affixes we use—*e.g., ism, asm, ics, ize, ist,* impart still more of a foreign, artificial character. Lastly, as said before, the natural rhythm of the English language, though Teutonic, is individual, and differs from that of the Anglo-Saxon, or of the German. An English sentence forced to assume the Latin rhythm strikes us at once as bookish and academic. The grammatical structure and the order of the words is Teutonic, though a few inversions are admissible or even pleasing. For all these reasons it is evident that English is not a composite or hybrid tongue compounded of Anglo-Saxon and Latin, but distinctly a Teutonic language, an organic growth from a vigorous national life. This point is emphasized at the risk of repetition, because it certainly is important that every one who is born to the use of a language should correctly appreciate its native character.

The Teutonic root of the English language has itself two branches, though not of equal importance. Before the Norman Conquest, which initiated the evolution of our modern tongue, the Saxon invaders of England were themselves subject to invasion by bands of Northern pirates whom they called Danes. These Danes made permanent settlements on the eastern coast, extended their ravages into the interior, and consolidated their power, till in the century before the Norman Conquest their chief, Knut, became king or overlord of England. They spoke old Norse, or Scandinavian, a language allied to the Low-Germanic tongues of the Angles and Saxons. The affinity of their languages, and the juxtaposition and partial amalgamation of the peoples resulted in the survival in English of a number of words of Norse origin. When the Norse word and the Anglo-Saxon word for the same thing were not alike in sound—or at least sufficiently unlike not to be confounded in ordinary utterance—one would be retained in the Danish districts and the other in the Saxon districts. By degrees the meanings would be differentiated, and in the end the language would possess two

MINOR SOURCES OF ENGLISH WORDS. 99

Words with slightly different shades of meaning. Thus, *whole* comes from the Anglo-Saxon *hal* (entire), and *hale* (hearty) comes from the Norse* or Scandinavian *heill* (sound or entire). In many cases the sounds were alike but the meanings different, and the result would be a pair of homonyms (words of the same sound but of different meanings). Thus, *fast* in the sense of firm, is English; but *fast* in the sense of rapid, is Norse. *Fast* to refrain from food, is a branch meaning of the former word, based on the idea that the abstainer is observing a firmly-established rule; but *fast asleep* comes from the second source, and means the state of sleeping rapidly, by rather an odd metaphor. Again, *flag*, to grow weary, is English; but *flag*, an ensign, is Norse; *aye*, meaning yes, is English; *aye*, meaning forever, is Norse; *bound*, secured or fastened, is English, but *bound*, in the sense of determined (bound to do it), is Norse. The same is true of *cow*, the animal, and *cow*, to dishearten; of *crab*, the crustacean, and *crab*, the fruit; and of many other pairs.

Many of the Norse derivatives are harsh and

---

* Old Norse is generally applied to Old West Norse only (Icelandic and Norwegian). Brugmann applies the term old Norse to the whole development of the Scandinavian languages up to the sixteenth century.—*Comparative Grammar*, § 10.

abrupt in sound, especially those beginning with the *sk* or *sh* sound. If we strike out *skate* and *skipper* (from the Dutch), *sk* in the beginning of a word is an almost sure mark of a Norse derivative. Words beginning with *sc* are about evenly divided between the English and the Norse groups, but the initial *sh* will be found about three times as often on an old English word as on one from the Norse.* Among the Norse words with the above initial letters are *scant, scald* (a poet, probably from same root as scold), *scar* (a rock), *scarf* (to hew diagonally), *scrip* (a bag), *scrape, scraggy, shoal, shingle, shunt*, etc. Many words of Norse origin end in *g*, as *drag, dreg, flag, hug, keg, slag, smug, rig, stag,* and *egg*.

There are about six hundred and sixty words in our language from the Norse, and three-fourths of them are monosyllables. The literary character of these words is about the same as that of the great body of those from the Anglo-Saxon. They are short and emphatic, often sibilant or guttural, and have a close relation to their meanings. They form a very valuable constituent part of our language because they are genuine folk-words, and entered it through oral speech, and therefore form one of the organic elements, and are not intruders like words that enter

* No Latin words begin with *sk*, and very few with *sc* or *sh*.

through the written language.* Many of them refer to maritime matters, and, as a rule, they have concrete—as opposed to abstract—meanings. The vigor of a language depends greatly on its wealth in words of concrete meaning, because we can always manufacture abstract terms from them. Concrete terms are the suggesters and feeders of thought.

The names of many villages in the parts of England inhabited by the Danes end in *bye* or *by*, or even *bee*. This syllable is from the Norse word for town or home. Thus we find Grimsby, Whitby, Netherby, Derby, etc. The laws of these towns or settlements were called *bye-laws*, a term we have retained for special rules. The word *bye* still means home or safe place in many games, and it is a Norse survival when children shout "Touch my *bye* first." Traces of Danish occupation can also be found in the names of towns ending in *ford* or *forth*, from Norse *fiord* (a bay), as in Waterford, Delforth, etc. The subject of geographical names will be touched on hereafter.

We have now run over briefly the sources of English words proper—that is, of words which came into the language during its formative period, and through the channel of general usage.

* A few words entered English from the Norse through the French. Such are *abet, brandish, bandage, blemish*. For a full list see *Skeat's Dictionary*, p. 750.

Several minor groups of words are found in modern English which have been borrowed from other languages. Some of them have come through the oral and some through the literary language. Some have been borrowed directly, and some after having been taken into a third language. Of these we will instance only the Greek, the Arabic, the Hebrew, and the Dutch group. A full review would name also the sporadic words — hardly numerous enough to be classified into groups — from the North American Indian, the Hindustanee, the Malayan, the American Spaniards, the Portuguese, and the languages of other peoples with whom the aggressive commercial instinct of the English has brought them in contact. These words are fully classified in *Skeat's Etymological Dictionary*, pp. 757-761.

An interesting group of words — interesting from the historical stand-point at least — is that which has come to us from the Arabic, usually from the language spoken by the Saracenic conquerors of Spain, commonly known as the Moors. Their civilization was marked by intellectual intensity as well as by artistic feeling. They were the mediæval pioneers in medicine and science, and many of the older chemical, astronomical, and mathematical terms are taken from their tongue. Among these are such words as *zenith*, *nadir*, and *azimuth;* the names of fixed stars, as

Aldebaran, Antares, Algol, Altair, Betelgeuse, Rigel, Fomalhaut, etc. All of these names have meanings, and frequently embody a poetic image.

That these Moors read Greek is shown not only by their treatises on Greek philosophy, but by the fact that many scientific terms are derived by us from them which were first borrowed by them from the Greek. Frequently they are compounded of the Arabic definite article *al* and some Greek term. *Alchemy*, for instance, is made up of this article and the Greek word meaning mingling; *alembic*, of the article and the Greek word meaning a cup. *Algebra*, too, is Arabic, and consists of the article and the first word of an expression meaning "the putting together and comparing," as is done in an equation. *Alkali* is pure Arabic, and means "the ashes," and took its meaning from the discovery that the ashes of sea-weed possess certain properties due to the presence of potash and soda. *Kali* also gives us *K* as the symbol of potash. *Alcohol* in Arabic means "the fine powder," and was supposed to be of magical efficacy. The transference of meaning to rectified spirit is comparatively modern.

We owe to these Moors also the great gift of simple characters for the numerals up to nine, and for the decimal notation which fixes values for these characters according to position on a scale of ten. How valuable an invention this was can be readily determined by learning to add or multiply numbers expressed in the clumsy Roman notation. The words *cipher* and *zero* come from the same Arabic term, *sifr*. The old Latin treatises on arithmetic wrote it *zephyrum*. The Italians contracted this into *zefiro*, and we shortened it still further into *zero*. But the French contracted the Latin word into *cifre*, and from them we took the form *cipher*. The two words have different meanings in English now, *zero* meaning nothing, or the starting-point of graduation on a scale, and *cipher* meaning the character. The word meant in Arabic empty or hollow before it was applied to the character.

Other words of Arabic origin which entered the English language by a roundabout course through some Romance language are *naphtha, rose, jasper, nitre, amulet, mattress, saffron, sultan, sofa, syrup,* and *candy*. *Admiral* is from *Emir al bahr*, lord of the sea. We took this word from the French, and at first spelled it *ammiral*. The Arabic group numbers about one hundred words, and their derivations are full of suggestions of Oriental history. Emerson called words "fossil poetry," and Trench observes that they are "fossil history," as well. *Admiral* carries us back to the time when a Moorish sea-captain was lord of the Mediterranean Sea, and Gibraltar (*Gebel al Tarik*, or Tarik's hill) was the landing-place of the conqueror of Spain.

If our Teutonic civilization is greatly indebted intellectually to one Semitic civilization, it is still more indebted spiritually to another—the Hebrew. But as Western civilization has come into contact with Hebrew civilization only through a book, our language has received very few words from the Hebrew. The translation of the Bible necessitated the transference of a few Hebrew words for which no equivalents could be found in English. These number but thirty, and embrace such words as *alleluia, behemoth, cherub, cinnamon, ephod, jug, Messiah, sack, Satan, sabaoth, shibboleth*. But the Greeks had intercourse with the Hebrews and Phœnicians before the Christian era, so that a number of words were borrowed by the Greeks from them. *Alphabet, delta, iota* are words of Hebrew root which we have received through the Greek. Most of these Hebrew-Greek words went into Latin from Greek in the Latin translation of the Septuagint. Among these are *amen, manna, rabbi, Pharisee, Sabbath, Sadducee*, etc. The names of the seven archangels, Michael, Gabriel, Raphael, Uriel, Chamuel, Jophiel, and Zadkiel * are also Semitic.

---

* In some lists Azrael, Satan, and Ithuriel take the place of the last three.

There has always been considerable commercial intercourse between the English and their ancestral relatives in Holland. Antwerp, or "At the Wharf," was the principal market for English wool before manufacturing was established in England. Colonies of Flemish artisans settled in England at the invitation of the King, or fleeing from religious persecution. The Dutch have always been a seafaring people, and many of our maritime terms are traceable to their language. Among these are *ahoy, avast, ballast, belay, boom, duck* (sail-cloth), *hold, hoy, hull, lighter, linstock, marline, orlop, reef, skipper, splice, sloop, yacht, yawl.* The similarity of the languages allowed the ready transference of words, but it is possible that some of the above maritime terms may have existed in the English sailor-language from very early times, parallel with their survival in Dutch, but have been first printed or written in Dutch. *Sloop, yacht,* and *yawl* are unquestionably Dutch.

Hollanders and Englishmen sympathized in the religious questions brought into prominence by the Reformation, but these questions were discussed for the most part in Latin. Otherwise, the exchange of some words of a more elevated character than the above might have resulted. The few words introduced into our language by the Dutch settlers of New York, like *stoop* (for portico), *crullers, supawn,** have never attained complete naturalization.

When we need a new scientific or mechanical word we are very apt to manufacture it from the Greek, as was done in the case of *telegraph, telephone, phonograph, dynamo, thermodynamic, isothermal,* and the numerous "ologies." A large number of scientific terms, especially those used in mathematics and geology, and many political and philosophical words, came from the Greek by natural transference. Aristotle, Euclid, Pythagoras, and Plato furnished our forefathers with thoughts and with terms for the thoughts. These cover such words as *analyze, anapest, dactyl, aphorism, axiom, category, hexagon,* and *climax.* The list of words taken directly from Greek is quite a long one — at least three hundred and fifty; but they are nearly all special words. More generally useful is the greater number that come from Greek through Latin, or through French through Latin. Many theological, literary, and poetic words are in these classes. We may instance of the first: *abyss, alms, angel, atom, asylum, echo, epoch, ethic, fungus, story, impolitic, orphan.* Of the second: *agony, air, austere, blame, cheer, diadem, giant, idiot, jealous, logic, machine, music, ocean, phrase, tyrant,*

---

* *Supawn* is Indian rather than Dutch, though used by the Dutch settlers.

trophy, tomb, tone, zeal, etc. It is evident that English has enriched itself from many sources. There is not one of these words that we would be willing to part with. Though in some cases they retain a slight scholastic flavor, they are thoroughly embedded in our speech, and are now just as truly English as are our words of undoubted Saxon ancestry.

The following tables are taken principally from those in Marsh's *Lectures on the English Language.* The first is based on the number of words, counting each word but once. For instance, after counting the word *is* once, it would not be allowed to enter the enumeration again, although it might occur a hundred times in the matter under consideration. In making the second table, however, the words *is, the, an,* etc., are counted every time they are used. The first is called an "enumeration of the total vocabulary;" the second is called an "enumeration of the total words used." The reason for the great preponderance of Teutonic words in the second table is, of course, that the particles, auxiliary verbs, and words of commonest use are Saxon, although our entire vocabulary is more than half Romance.

The relative percentage of Latin words in the Bible and in Milton are especially worthy of comparison.

MINOR SOURCES OF ENGLISH WORDS. 109

TOTAL VOCABULARY, 100.

NAME OF BOOK OR WRITER.	Per cent. of Anglo-Saxon Words.
The Ormŭlum, A.D. 1225 (semi-Saxon)	97
English Bible	60
Shakspeare	60
Milton (poetry)	33

TOTAL WORDS USED, INCLUDING REPETITIONS, 100.

NAME OF BOOK OR WRITER.	Per cent. of Anglo-Saxon Words.
Robert of Gloucester, ten pages	96
Piers' Ploughman, Introduction, entire	88
Chaucer, Prologue, 420 verses	88
Squire's Tale, entire	91
Sir Thomas More, seven pages	84
Faerie Queen, one canto	86
John's Gospel, four chapters	96
Matthew's Gospel, three chapters	93
Romans, four chapters	90
Othello, Act V	89
Tempest, Act I	88
Milton, L'Allegro	90
" Il Penseroso	83
" Paradise Lost	80
Addison, Spectator	82
Pope, poetry	80
Swift, Political Lying	88
" John Bull	85
Johnson, Preface to Dictionary	72

NAME OF BOOK OR WRITER.	Per cent. of Anglo-Saxon Words.
Junius, two letters	76
Hume's History, one chapter	73
Gibbon, Decline and Fall, one chapter.	70
Webster,* Second Speech on Foote's Resolution	75
Irving, Stout Gentleman	85
" Westminster Abbey	77
Macaulay, Essay on Lord Bacon	75
Channing, Essay on Milton	75
Cobbett, on Indian-corn	80
Prescott, one chapter	77
Bryant, Death of the Flowers	92
" Thanatopsis	84
Mrs. Browning, Cry of the Children	92
" " Lost Bower	77
Robert Browning, Bishop Blougram's Apology	84
Edward Everett, Eulogy on Adams	76
Ticknor, History of Spanish Literature, one chapter	73
Tennyson, The Lotus-eaters	87
" In Memoriam, first twenty strophes	89

* Large Latin percentage owing to repetition of words like congress, constitution, union, etc. Webster ordinarily employed about eighty per cent. of Saxon words.

NAME OF BOOK OR WRITER.	Per cent. of Anglo-Saxon Words,
Ruskin, Modern Painters, chapter on the Superhuman Ideal	73
Longfellow, Miles Standish	87
Martineau, Endeavors after the Christian Life	74

We see from the above that after the language was first made a literary vehicle by Chaucer, down to the middle of the eighteenth century, the proportion of Saxon words used by the best writers was not far from seventeen words, counting repetitions, to three of the foreign classes, and that Shakspeare and the Bible are markedly Saxon; that after this period the proportion increased, reaching the maximum of Latinity in Gibbon; that during the present century there has been a reversion to the use of Saxon, especially marked in poetry; and that the subject-matter influences the number of Saxon words used. This last is shown by the different ratios given by Milton's "L'Allegro," where the thought is cheerful and superficial, and the images drawn for the most part from rural life; and by his "Il Penseroso" (the reflective man), the tone of which is more philosophical, and the images scholastic or social. Again, " Westminster Abbey " naturally suggests topics connected with history and chivalry, and the writer draws more freely on our store of Romance words. The "Stout Gentleman" is on a less dignified plane, and familiar Saxon phrases fit the thought. The same contrast is evident between Mrs. Browning's two poems, the "Cry of the Children" and the "Lost Bower." The modern reversion to Saxon words will be the more marked if we reflect that since Dr. Johnson's day the number of Saxon words in ordinary use has not increased materially, while a large number of alien terms have been made familiar by science and the arts. It is further noteworthy how Saxon our best poetry is, and how Latinized our philosophic and artistic criticism, as shown by Ruskin and Martineau. It seems strange, at first sight, that, as the table makes evident, an increase of only two or three per cent. in the number of Latin derivatives used should give the effect of excessive Latinity. Probably this is produced by the cadence and structure of the sentences more than by the character of the vocabulary.

CHAPTER X.

METHOD OF THE WORD-FORMING INSTINCT.

THE origin of language is shrouded in impenetrable mystery, like the origin of everything else. There can be no record before the means of making a record exist. By studying languages we can find out how they have changed during the historic period, and how they are changing now. We can then infer what the changes before that period must have been—proceed from the known to the unknown, on the hypothesis that the process by which languages were developed in the past 3000 years is the same by which they were developed in the much longer period during which articulate speech was slowly assuming the forms which we now recognize as the most archaic. This is all that we can do, and we run the risk of overlooking some factor of prime importance which has ceased to be operative. Again, we must remember that the part of the total development of language that has taken place in historic time is so slight in comparison with what had taken place before, that inferences carried from the nature of operations in the known past to those of the unknown past are very likely to be erroneous. The difference between a modern man and the most primitive man of whom we have record is small compared to the difference between the most primitive man and his earliest possible ancestor. Even if we should become convinced that the original word-forming instinct is still at work among modern men, we must remember that, like all the great primitive human instincts, it is so thwarted and corrupted by civilization that its original trend and character are barely discernible. Nor, for obvious reasons, does the process of acquiring the power of speech by infants throw much light — if any — on the original race-process. The powers and tendencies of the child are all inherited, and those which date from fifty or one hundred generations back are the controlling ones, to the exclusion of the primitive instincts, and, what is of more consequence, the modern child is born into a modern environment.

Since the discovery of Sanskrit a number of conclusions have been established by philologists. The great fact of the relationship of all the Aryan tongues points towards, if it does not establish, the unity of the race. The fact that all the Aryan languages are based on a limited number of roots or simple sounds about two hundred in number, most of which seem to be connected with a certain action, proves that language is a growth, in a fuller and more comprehensive sense than had before been thought possible, and shows, further, that man is a thinker just so far as he is in possession of words, and that both these powers must once have been in an elementary condition. Furthermore, it has been shown that language has been built on these roots by the use of metaphors. When the need was felt of expressing some new conception, an old word or combination of words was used which expressed a real or fancied resemblance between the thing already named and the new thing for which a name was wanted. Thus, man is a poet or maker of words in very much the same way that he is a creator of any poetical form. This metaphor-making power is the main force in the formation of language, and it is necessary to assume the possession of only a very elementary vocabulary for a starting-point. In the present chapter it is the intention to present evidences of this poetic imaginative faculty in some of our English words, the derivations of which are easily ascertained. It has been exercised in the formation of every word if we follow its history far enough back.

For instance, breath and air and wind having

names (probably one word), and a dead man or animal being one which has ceased to breathe, breath or air would naturally be thought to be that which constitutes life, or that which, having departed, made the living animal dead. Therefore, in all languages we find that the word which signifies soul or spirit has for a root the word signifying air or breath. Thus, spirit is *spiritus;* *animus* is Greek *anemos*, or wind. The origin of our word *soul* is unknown, but it may be taken for granted that it is some concrete and sensible thing used as the sign of an invisible thing. The Teutonic word *ghost* is from the root meaning breath.

When it is said that these primitive metaphors are poetical, it is not meant that they always are what we should recognize as poetically beautiful. They are frequently so, for they are nearly always apt illustrations of something abstract by something more concrete. It is the evidence of the naïve striving of primitive man with his limited stock of materials to express something just beyond him, that makes the roots of language poetical, for this struggling to express something not definitely understood is the main-spring of all art. Strange as it may appear, these primitive metaphors have widely colored our conceptions of spiritual things.

It may very naturally be objected that, if a few

verbal roots form the elements of primitive language, we should find some savage tribes, whose development is in the lowest possible condition, in possession of these roots and nothing more, whereas no such example can be found. The answer to this is that the world is very old, and that no savage tribe represents the condition of primitive man, for all savages show traces of great antiquity in their inherited instincts and superstitions. The infant, undeveloped racial man cannot be found, for it is too late. The modern savage is mature, though in a state of warped development, and behind him lie hundreds of centuries of torpid life before we reach the period — if ever there was such a period — when language was formed from its elements, and the original language - building power of humanity was exerted. Therefore, we must look on a savage tribe as a wreck quite as much as a germ, and can draw no better inferences from its speech than we can from the speech of a highly-developed community. We find, too, that savages, as far as they have risen to the conception of abstractions, have employed the same method of expressing them in speech that civilized men did.

Names, then, are never given arbitrarily, except by moderns. All the geographical names mentioned in the chapter on local names, if of any respectable antiquity, are real names—mean something, embody something. *Himalay* means the abode of snow. *Sneefell* and *Ben-Nevis* have the same signification—the snow mountain. *Sutherland* (the *South*land), the north-west county of Scotland, is so called because the name was given by the Norse inhabitants of the islands to the north of it. England, or Angle-land, is called *Albion* on account of the white chalk cliffs of the southern coast as seen from the Continent. Even now if a folk-name is allowed to form itself, it grows from some root in the same way that the earliest ones did.

The names of flowers not unfrequently embody a rustic poetry. Chaucer's *daisy* is the eye of day. *Buttercup* and *golden-rod* are equally descriptive. *Rosemary* is *ros marine*, from some fancied resemblance between the flower and sea spray. It has been altered from *ros marine* by reason of a popular etymology connecting it with rose of Mary. *Rose* is from an Arabic word which passed into Greek, thence into Latin, thence into English. *Foxglove* embodies a pretty conceit. The *asters* have a star-like form. *Geranium* is from the Greek *geranos*, a crane, the flowers having a fancied resemblance to a stork's bill in color. *Pink* comes from a Celtic word meaning to pierce, as in "to pink with a rapier," and the name was given on account of the "pinked" or serrated edges of the flowers. *Mallow* is from a Latin word based on *mollis*, soft. Through the French it gives us *mauve*, the color. The *violet* also has given its name to a shade of blue. *Lilac* was the Persian name of the indigo plant, but, being appropriated in English to a flowering shrub with purple blossoms, has given its name to a shade of light purple. *Bud* is from a word meaning to push. *Nasturtium* is supposed to be from *nas-torquere* (nose-twister). *Daffodil* is from Greek, *asphodel*. *Wort* is the Saxon word for plant, and *dock* is the Celtic. In consequence, these words appear very frequently in the folk-names for plants and herbs.

Primitive metaphors are very well illustrated in the words for feelings and actions of the mind. Thus, *attention* is a stretching of the mind. *Tension*, as applied to a mental state, is of modern coinage, but is based on much the same metaphorical conception. Our modern notions of physical science have given to this word and to *pressure* a new meaning. *Conception (con ca₫pio)*, a taking of two things together, or of one thing with another,* is based on the idea that in an

* It is quite possible that the original force of the Latin prefix *con* or *cum* was not taking two things together, but taking all parts of a thing at once. *Comprehend* and *conceive* would then mean grasping the whole of a thing, not grasping a thing with its attendant circumstances. But the fact that the original metaphorical transfer lay in using a physical action to express a mental action remains un-

elementary mental act we compare one thing with another. One cannot *comprehend* anything unless it is taken hold of *with* its associated ideas. *Associated* ideas are companion thoughts, from *socius*. *Idea* is from the root *vid*, to see. An idea is a mental image. To see with the eye and to know with the mind are analogous. *Sympathy*, from the Greek, and *compassion*, from the Latin, express the thought that when we sympathize or compassionate in the true sense, we share suffering with another person. *Passion* is from *patior*, to suffer, as if a man in a passion were enduring the mastery of a demon. The old use means suffering; from the same root are *pathos, patient*, and *passive*. *Anger* and *anguish, awe*, and even *quinsy* are all from the same root, *AGH*, to choke. *Courage* is from *cœur*, the heart. *Hate* is based on the same root as *hunt*, meaning to pursue. *Love* is from a root meaning to covet, to desire. This would seem to show that hate was recognized as an active principle earlier than love, since its root contains a less complex idea, though such an inference borders on the fanciful.

Mental states and characteristics are expressed by condensed metaphors. *Modest* signifies a

changed. This is the point in which the growth of language illustrates the development of the human intellect from lower views to higher ones.

person who acts within a *modus*, or rule, and the root *MA*, from which it comes, gives us also *measure* and *moon*, and, possibly, *man*. The radical idea in the word *temper* is to moderate or qualify by mixing. This original import of the word is seen in the phrase to *temper* mortar, or to *temper* steel, for in tempering steel something was supposed to mix or unite with the metal so as to harden it. Again, *temperature* was taken to mean degree or amount of heat, in accordance with the theory that something material mixed with a substance to make it hot. *Temper* as applied to the disposition meant the state resulting from a mixture of moods or impulses. Originally, it was implied that the resulting state was a proper and commendable one, but now when we say a "fit of *temper*" we mean a fit of bad temper. The use of the *talents* for mental aptitudes comes, of course, from the parable of the intrusted talents or sums of money. The adjective *talented* was objected to in the last generation, but seems to have acquired a good standing now, though it is better to avoid using it. At all events it has expelled the word *gifted*. The original root of the word *memory* is not known. It would probably mean something like picking up, or sorting out, or seeing a second time. But the verb *think* is supposed to be distantly connected with the root of the word *thing*, as if the thought were originally regarded as an image or emanation of the thing thought of. *Lunacy* derives its name from the superstition that the mental condition was somehow influenced by the moon, though the common word *loony** is based on a metaphor drawn from the Norse word, *loon*, which in Iceland may refer to a foolish bird, though in our country it signifies one quite as intelligent as those who try to shoot it. The point to notice in all these cases is that a concrete thing is always found to be the godfather of an abstraction in the early efforts of man to express himself, and that his progress has been from the conception of the material to the partial conception of the spiritual. We are so closely bound to matter that we cannot learn to think without using the

---

* The names of birds, with the exception of *duck*, are used in a derogatory sense when applied to human beings, to carry the idea that a person resembles the bird in undesirable qualities—*e.g.*, *coot, goose, peacock, owl, loon, gull, booby. Loon* in the expression "crazy as a *loon*" has been influenced in its meaning by the word *lunatic* from Latin *luna*, which was applied to persons whose sanity was temporarily disturbed under the impression that the changes of the moon were somehow responsible for periods of mental derangement. For this reason *loony* is sometimes incorrectly spelled *luny*. The old word *loon* or *loom* is also applied to an awkward clown ("Macbeth," Act. V., Scene iii., line xi.). *Booby*, too, is probably primarily an epithet applied to a man, and connected with *balbutier*, to stammer, and afterwards given to a bird in a derisive sense.

words which represented matter in man's earliest speech.

So great is the influence of our material surroundings on us that, had we lived as fishes do in a gross medium like water, perhaps we should never have risen to the conception of pure spirit. The rarer medium, the ether, through which heat and light are conveyed, is not perceptible by our senses. Hence it has never been so fruitful of words to express conceptions of mental and spiritual being as has air. *Fiery* is an old word, but it is not based on the word meaning fire, and does not radically mean a conflagration in the mind, but simply a rapid movement. When we say an "illuminated intellect," or an "ethereal being," we are using comparatively modern metaphors; but the word *spirit*, from breath or air, is so ancient a metaphor that we have ceased to be conscious that it is one. Nevertheless, the formation of all of these metaphors is due to an effort of the word-building instinct.

There is another element, of comparatively little importance, in the word-building instinct, and that is the tendency to imitate the thing signified by the vocal sound which represents it. Thus, *buzz, whiz, crack, roar, creak, croak, crash, boom, hiss, hum, howl* (probably), *roar, squeak, drum, tomtom,* and *fizz* are imitative words. As these words are original, it has been thought that they were entitled to rank as roots, and that language might have sprung from an attempt to reproduce certain of the natural sounds or noises. If we suppose man to have once been an animal destitute of language but possessed of the power of acquiring it, and eagerly desirous of communicating with his fellows, it is difficult to imagine what he could have done except to gesture and make imitative noises, just as persons do now when they cannot speak the same language. But can we assume an analogy between speechless man and modern man without being misled by it? And why should man not have developed a sign language instead of a vocal language? Max Müller ridicules the theory that language may have originated in attempts to imitate the sounds of nature as the *bow-wow* theory. The serious objections to it are: First, the onomatopœic words, with one or two exceptions, are not the fruitful words, the generative sounds, by the compounding and modification of which whole groups are formed. *Hiss* and *buzz* are two very good examples of onomatopœic words, but they are destitute of progeny; while from *sta*, to stand, is derived a family of at least ten different groups, and *spak*, to see, has been still more productive. Second, the imitative words are quite different in closely-allied languages, showing that they are of comparatively late origin. Third, the number of things and actions which can be represented by a characteristic sound is quite limited, and entirely inadequate to form the basis of language.

It is true that there are a few onomatopœic roots, or rather roots having some onomatopœic quality, like *bahl*, to resound, the root of bellow, bawl, and bull; *gu*, to low, the root of *cow;* *mu*, to mutter, the root of *mutter;* and *mur*, the root of *murmur*, all of which refer to sounds; but even these are not the great fruitful roots from which language draws its nourishment.* Again, there is a large number of words like *breeze*, *thunder*, *freeze*, *grind*, *tear*, etc., of which we think the sound expressive of the sense, they are so closely related in our minds. Possibly in the wear and tear of, time the onomatopœic sense of man may have modified the sound of these words slightly, but in their originals no resemblance between sense and sound can be found. On the whole, we should say that any pair of them might change meanings even now without any loss of fitness. We therefore allow to the onomatopœic or imitative propensity a very subordinate part in language-formation, and recognize the imaginative or metaphor-suggesting power of the human thinker as

* For a full and plausible presentation of the arguments sustaining the theory that language sprang from imitations of natural sounds, see Canon Farrar's book, *Language and Languages*.

the building energy of word-growth. It is true this last does not account for the origin of the roots. It takes these for granted, and so must any rational theory of language.

At present, when a name is sought for a new thing or operation, it is arbitrarily manufactured. The botanists go to the Latin dictionary, the physicists to the Greek. There is no invention in this, no word-creating. It is merely ransacking the lumber-room for a disused tool and using it over again. In this way we have *telescope*, the far-seer; *telegraph*, the far-writer; *telephone*,* the distant-speaker; *stereoscope*, the solid-seer, and thousands of others. The verb telescope, as applied to a train of cars that have been forced into each other, is a happy example of the metaphorical word-making power in modern days. It is an indigenous growth out of a manufactured word. So also is the use of the word *photograph* for the quick fixing of a mental image on the memory. A long time is required for these artificial words to become fully naturalized in the language, though they are very necessary for the naming of new devices. Multitudes of them drop out or remain entombed in our dictionaries alongside of many of the barbarous Latin words of the seventeenth and eighteenth centuries. Some of the coined words

* And yet we say "long-distance telephone," or long-distance long-distance speaker.

of science are very happy inventions; as, *atavism*, to express the mysterious appearance in an individual of some mark of his remote ancestors, and, *isothermals*, lines drawn through points when the mean annual temperatures are the same. The conceptions of modern science are gradually coloring our thought, and the scientific terminology, if apt and striking, must more and more enter our daily speech.

The foregoing are words which enter the language at the top and work down. Another class take the natural course of entering at the bottom and taking their chances. These are the words of indigenous growth, or *slang*. Sometimes they are coined, but not unfrequently they spring from an expressive folk-metaphor.* Multitudes of them die yearly, though they may have a vigorous life for a while. No one can tell whether any given slang-word will survive. *Dude* and *crank* are valuable words, and each denotes something not signified by any other English word. Ten years from this time they may be out of use, or

* Victor Hugo says (*Les Misérables*): "Slang is a vestibule where language disguises itself when it has some crime to commit. It puts on these masks of words, these rags of metaphors." This applies to an *Argot*, or slang dialect. Teutonic slang is language too full of rude, boisterous life. It expresses the humorous, not the criminal, attitude towards life. It is a sign of linguistic health and vivacity. It reflects national character.

they may be in as good standing as *mob*, once a slang-word. *Crank*,* a metaphor from *cranky*, an unstable craft, if it can establish itself, will prove a valuable acquisition and save many a tedious circumlocution. The *dude* of 1890 is so different from the *dandy* of 1840, and the word is so expressive of one aspect of the genius of our age that it ought to be saved, but probably it will "have to go." *Swell*, originally from "swell mob," is also expressive and seems to be making its way. *Rattled*, demoralization accompanied by alarm, is also a good folk-metaphor. It may become respectable and literary. These indigenous growths have far more of the genius of the language than have the scientific formations. Nevertheless, they must be received with circumspection, for ninety in a hundred are ephemeral. The word *slang* itself is comparatively modern, and originated in a slang expression connected with sling. Now it is an indispensable word, if not strictly literary.

* The entrance of *crank* into literary society would seem to be signalized by its appearance in the title of an article in the *Atlantic Monthly* (September, 1890) : "Cranks as Social Motors." Max Müller's *Science of Language* (Second Series, Lecture viii.) contains a suggestive disquisition on this subject—the extension of the meaning of words by metaphorical use until the metaphor is forgotten.

CHAPTER XI.

GROUPS OF WORDS WITH A COMMON ROOT.

To group words under their original Proto-Aryan roots implies more philological knowledge than is assumed for the readers of this book. But in every language there are families of words springing from the same root in that language. This relationship can be profitably examined by any one, since it illustrates on a small scale what may be called word-branching, the process by which words, sometimes apparently unrelated in meaning, grow out of the same root. What could at first sight be more distinct in idea than the word *post* in *post*-haste and in fence-*post*. Yet they are the same in origin. Let us examine a few groups of English words thus related. We will take up the words connected with *check*, *quatuor* (four), *stick*, *post*, *stem*, *do*, and a few others. Skeat's smaller *Etymological Dictionary*, which groups words by their root-relationships, contains a great deal of information on this subject in a compact form.

Check is derived from the game of chess, which is of Persian or Indian origin, and is much older than the English language. "*Ex oriente lux et ludus scaccorum.*" *Check-mate* is *shah mat*, the king is dead, and *check* is *shah*—that is, look out for the king. From this came readily the meaning of a sudden repulse, a stop, as in *check-rein*, *check-valve*, to meet with a *check*.

Chess, the game, is *shahs*, *shaks* or checks, and means the battle of the kings.

Checker-board, or *chess-board*, is the board of alternate squares on which the game is played.

The table on which the accounts of the king's treasurer were kept was called a checker-board or exchequer, because it was painted with squares of different colors. The squares were used for the purpose of computation, perhaps with the aid of counters. The place, therefore, was known as the "court of exchequer," the *e* being euphonic before *s* and *x*, as in *escheat, estoppel*, etc. The treasury department is still called *the exchequer*, in consequence.

Check, a written order for money deposited, sometimes pedantically spelled *cheque*, was originally either an exchequer bill or draft on the treasury, or else connected with the idea of a check or restraint on the paying out of money by the one to whom it is intrusted.

The derivatives of *quatuor* bear their origin on

their faces. A *quadrangle* has four angles, and a *quadrant* is the fourth part of a circle. *Quadrille* is a game at cards for four persons or a dance for four couples. *Quaternions* is a branch of mathematics which proceeds as if there were four dimensions. *Quarry* is a place where stones are worked square. A *quadroon* has one-quarter negro blood; a *quadruped* has four feet; a *quart* is a quarter of a gallon; a *quarto* is a sheet folded into four leaves; a *squadron* and a *squad* is a body of troops in a square—a square has four sides. In all these words except *quarry* the idea of four parts is very evident, and the branching has not proceeded very far.

From *pono*, besides the compounds *deposit*,* *expound*, *impost*, etc., we have the word *post* in several quite different senses. Thus, to *post a sentry* means to assign him a definite position; but *post*, in
  "Thousands at his bidding haste,
   And *post* o'er land and sea,"
and in
  "My days are swifter than a *post*,"

* It is odd enough that a large number of words containing *pose*—all that come from the French—*pose, compose, dispose, expose, propose, purpose, repose, suppose,* and *transpose,* are not from *pono* but from *pausare*, to bring to rest; but everything connected with the sb. *position*, like *deponent* or *supposition*, comes direct from the Latin *pono* (position). Two Latin verbs were confused in France.

evidently means to move rapidly. *Post-office, fence-post*, *to post a ledger*, *post-haste*, *post-chaise*, have all grown out of the idea of position. Thus the fence-post is fixed in the ground, the military post is established at a certain place, items are placed or posted in the ledger; the post-offices, also, were established at fixed points; the post-chaise was drawn by horses kept at the posts; and to post a letter and to post in the sense of riding rapidly are evidently derived from the post in post-office.

Stick is a word whose relationship takes in a great many words. There are really two verbs, *stick*, to pierce, and *stick*, to be fixed fast. A butcher speaks of *sticking a hog*, and a wagoner of *sticking in the mud*. The active and the transitive verb, though evidently different words, are confounded in modern English, though the connection between piercing and holding fast is evidently remote. *Sting* is the same as *stick*, to pierce, but has retained its identity. From this double word *stick* come *tick, ticket, etiquette, stack, stake, steak, stick* (sb.), *stitch, stock, stocking*, and *stoker*. *Ticket* and *etiquette* come through the French from the German, and are therefore distant connections. A ticket was originally a little bill or order stuck up on the gate of a court; hence etiquette, a rule of social conduct. *Tick*, credit, came from the practice of buying things without paying for them, and having the charge marked on a card which was stuck up. A memorandum-book of charges is thus still known as "a tickler," and the cashier, when he takes money from the drawer, substitutes, or should substitute, a "ticket." *Stack* is a pile stuck up—that is, held fast. A *stake* may be something stuck fast in the ground, or it may be a sharp piece of wood to pierce the ground. (We say a horse staked himself when he is wounded by a piece of wood.) A *beefsteak* is a bit of meat stuck on the point of a fork. A *stick* is a small bit of wood, so called from its piercing or sticking into anything. A printer's stick may be the holder in which the types are stuck, but more probably is connected with *sto*, to stand, and corrupted. A *stake* is money held fast. *Stock*, originally that which is held fast, as the stock or stem of a tree, has a great variety of secondary meanings, as family stock, the stem of the family tree, live-stock, that which is fixed to the farm, the stock of a gun in which the barrel is fixed. Fixed or invested capital is also stock. The machine in which a malefactor's legs were fastened was called the *stocks*. The connection of *stockings* and of *stock*, the stiff construction once worn about the neck by men, does not seem so clear. A *stoker* cleans his fire by sticking a long poker into it, and a *stickleback* is a fish with a stick, or something to pierce, on his back. As the *st* appears in all these words, we may note how much more obstinate a thing a consonant is than a vowel. The combination *st* seems to stand the wear and tear of use remarkably well.

In the Norse tongues was a word *heil* or *hel*, and in the Anglo-Saxon a word *hal*, both meaning, substantially, whole, entire, both distantly related to the Greek καλος, beautiful, complete. From one or the other of these—they are really the same word, though one may have been the origin of an English word in one part of the country and the other in another part—come *hale*, *hail* (a greeting), *whole, heal, health, holy, hallow, halibut, holiday, hollyhock*, and *wassail. Wassail* was Anglo-Saxon *Wes-hal*, be well (your health!), and was a pledge or drinking of health at a feast. *Hollyhock* is the holy mallow, so called because it was brought from Palestine. *Halibut* is the *holy but* or flounder, a fish which the Church allowed its votaries to eat on fast-days. The connection between holiness or perfection on the one hand, and health or physical completeness on the other, is quite evident, as is also the connection between *hail*, a greeting, and the original meaning. *Halloo* has no connection with *hal*, though the sound, or rather the spelling, suggests that it might have. It is from an Anglo-Saxon interjection, *eala*, and is confounded with the Norman call, *Hola*, or Ho there! the form used by Shakspeare.

Another prolific root-word is the base of the Anglo-Saxon *sceran*, and of the equivalent Norse word meaning to shear. Thus we have *shear, jeer, scar* (a rock), *scare, score, shard, shred, share, sheer, shire, sheriff, shore, shore* (a prop), *short, shirt, skirt*—all of the same family. Notice the obduracy of the consonant sound in this instance, and that the Norse members of the connection begin with *sk*, and the Anglo-Saxon with *sh*. The relation of signification is sufficiently evident, except, perhaps, in the case of *jeer*, which Skeat gives as from a Dutch phrase meaning to shear the fool, *i.e.*, to jest at one. *Score*, meaning twenty, comes from the practice of keeping count by notches on a stick, as Robinson Crusoe kept his diary. A deeper notch was made at twenty. Axemen still score a piece of timber before they "hew to the line," and we keep the score of a game. The *shire* is territory divided from the rest, and the *shire-reeve* is the executive officer. The *shore* is the dividing line between land and water. When a vessel *sheers* off she cuts the water at an angle. A *shore* is a prop cut to the proper length, a *ploughshare* cuts the earth, and a *share* of stock is a part separated or cut off. So with *shred* and *shard*. A *shirt* is a truncated garment, and a *skirt* is cut round the bottom. To *skirt* along the shore means, perhaps, to make short cuts from point to point. *Scare* is more remotely connected in meaning, as it derives from Norse *skerre*, timid, shy, which is based on the idea of sheering off. This group of words illustrates the double Teutonic source—Norse and Low German —of the modern English.

Do, to perform, comes from an Anglo-Saxon word, as does also *do*, to be worth, to avail. The use of the first as an emphatic auxiliary, as in "I do say so," "I do not think so," is comparatively modern. From this comes *ado, to-do, deed, deem, doom, doof, dup* (to do off and to do up), *indeed*, and *deemster* (a judge). From *do*, to avail, comes *doughty* (valiant). "How do you do?" is a very odd idiom when we examine it. "How actualize you in practicable availability?" is about the substance of our daily salutation.

Latin words have branched in the original language, and also since their naturalization in English. Much of this is due to suffixes and prefixes—compounding rather than growth. *Ducere* to lead; *tangere*, to touch; *dicere*, to say; and *agere*, to perform, are familiar examples. From *duco* come *duke, abduction, conduce, conduct* (in both senses), *conduit, douche* (a shower-bath, since the water is brought through a *duct*), *doge, ducat, ductile, educate, introduce, redoubt* (an intrenchment to which to lead the men back), *reduce, subdue, traduce* (to lead a reputation to dishonor), etc.

From *tango* come *tangent, contain, contagious,*

integer (a whole, intact), *tact* (a delicate touch), *taste*, and *tax*, of which last the original meaning was primarily to handle, hence to value, to appraise.

From *dico* come *diction*, *abdicate*, *addict*, *condition*, *contradict*, *dedicate*, *dictionary*, *ditto* (what has been said), *ditty*, *edict*, *indicate*, *index*, *indite*, *preach* (*predicare*), *predicate* (in two senses), and *predict*. In all of these the connection of meaning is sufficiently evident.

From *agere* we have *agent* and *act*, *agile*, *agitate*, *ambiguous*, *coagulate*, *cogent*, *cogitate*, *enact*, *exact*, *transact*, and others more remote; in all of which we see the idea of effective agency.

The relationship of meaning in words from the Latin is usually very evident, though the form is sometimes disguised in coming through the French. In *miscreant*, originally unbeliever, and in *recreant*, one false to faith, the *credo* is disguised. So in *defy*, to proclaim all bonds of faith broken, the *fides* does not appear. *Frontispiece*, again, is not connected with piece, but with *specio*, and means something to be looked at in the beginning. In *preface*, from *præfatio*, the root is *fari*, to speak, not *facio*, to do. Of disguised forms something will be said hereafter. The English roots, however, have been much longer under the influence of phonetic changes, and, perhaps, are more susceptible to them. A few more instances, in no case exhaustive, will finish this branch of the subject.

Beatan, to strike, gives us *bat*, *beetle* (a wooden maul), and *batter*, a kind of pudding beaten up.

Beorgan, to shelter, besides its connection with *burough*, already spoken of, gives us *burglar* (probably corrupted from *burgh* and *latro*), *harbinger* (one who precedes to procure a harbor), *harbor*, and *cold harbor*. A cold harbor was an inn where the traveller could procure shelter but no cooking. There are a number of places in England still called Cold Harbour, and one or two in this country.

Blawan, to blow, is the origin of *bladder*, of *blaze*, to proclaim after giving notice with a horn. We still speak of a blaze on a tree (a mark which proclaims a boundary), *blare* (of a trumpet), *blister*, and *bloat*. Skeat says, however, that the connection between *blow* and *bloat* is conjectural. *Blatant* and *bleat* plainly belong here.

From *brynen*, to burn, comes *brown, brimstone, brandy, brand*, and *brindled*. Skeat places *brunt* here, as if the brunt of the battle was connected with a burning or hot fight, which seems odd enough.

From *ceapian*, to buy, we have our word *cheap, chapman, chaffer;* and in composition, *Cheapside* and *Copenhagen*, the merchan's haven. Since buying necessitates trading or exchange, we have *chop* in the phrases "to chop logic," and "the wind *chops*" or changes its direction. The result is a "chopping sea." In this last we have gone some distance from the idea of purchase, but each step is logical.

Daelian, to divide, is found in the phrase "a good *deal*," a considerable part; *dole*, a portion of food given in charity; *deal*, a piece of wood and to *deal* the cards. Distantly connected are *dale* and *dell*, a division or cleft in the hills.

Wyrt, an herb, appears in wort—St. John's *wort*, etc.; in *wart*, a growth on the finger; in *orchard*, or *wort-yard*. Orchard could not come from *hortus*, a garden, because the last syllable must be accounted for.

Our large modern dictionaries give the etymologies of words so fully that these few examples are quoted merely to incite the reader to look up others for himself. Take the following words: *wit, war, wade, tell, shoot, pike, mow, batch, bear, can, food, clover, know, dray*, and note their connections, some of which are very peculiar. There is no branch of the subject in which conjecture is more apt to be misleading than in accounting for the different meanings of words similar in sound. Long experience sometimes fails to impart a trustworthy judgment, so capricious seems the popular method of transferring meanings. In default of an historical sequence great caution is necessary, but sometimes not observed.

CHAPTER XII.

ERRONEOUS DERIVATIONS.

ETYMOLOGISTS are far from being infallible. The usual causes of mistakes are excessive ingenuity and disregard of the method in which the human mind works in forming a language and in transferring the meaning of words from one thing to another, or else ignorance of the way in which old sounds and spellings have been modified. Thus Dr. Thomas Fuller, a man of sense and acuteness, says: "As for those that count the Tartars the offspring of the ten tribes of Israel which Shalmanasar led away captive, because Totari signifyeth in the Hebrew and Syriac tongue a residue, or remnant, learned men have sufficiently confuted it. And surely it seemeth a forced and overstrained deduction to farre fetch the name of Tartars from a Hebrew word, a language so far distant from them."

"The theory of Fuller," says Professor Marsh, "was better than his practice, for he derives *compliment* from *completi mentiri*, and not from *com-*

pletio mentis, because compliments are usually completely mendacious."* Elsewhere he quotes, with seeming assent, Sir John Harrington's ridiculous derivation of the old English *elf* and *goblin* from the two great political families, Guelf and Ghibbeline. Thus, also, *abominable*, which is evidently derived from the Latin *ab* and *omen*, and involves the notion of what is religiously profane and detestable—"the abominations of the heathen," for example—was supposed to be derived from *ab* and *homo*, as if it signified something inhuman. For a long time it was spelled *abhominable*, in accordance with this forced derivation, and though the error in the spelling has not been perpetuated, the word itself has taken up the meaning of something repugnant to humanity and not merely sacrilegious.

The word *Amazon* is frequently given as compounded of *a*, primitive, and *mazon* (Greek), the breast, with the explanation that the tribe of female warriors which bore the name, cut off their left breasts to acquire greater facility in drawing the bow. This is so evidently absurd that the error is repeated in our dictionaries simply because no one has made a better guess at the derivation.

* Compliment and complement (math.) are both *completement*, or filling up. Extending courtesies, flattery, complying with wishes, is a meaning easily derived from "filling up."

Mariposa, the Spanish for butterfly, is sometimes referred to *mare*, the sea, and *posa*, position or rest, because the insect flutters aimlessly and then alights, and the sea is sometimes in motion and sometimes quiet. Anything more flatly sentimental than this derivation cannot easily be imagined. It has not even the merit of being a really poetical invention.

Again, the word *pie* is referred in Webster to *pastry* by a desperate guess. By this method all words beginning in *p* and of similar meaning would be connected. But words are connected by some law which governs the relation of the different sounds and meanings, and not haphazard. The word *pie* is probably a Celtic word, like many of the elementary kitchen-words, and dates from the time when Celtic slaves performed the menial offices of the kitchen. The pie in *magpie* is another word connected with the Latin *picus*, a woodpecker.

Pie or *pi*, meaning a heap of type, probably comes from *pica*, the name of a certain size of type, which might be applied to an unassorted heap.

One source of absurd etymologies is the resemblance in the sound of words of different meanings in two languages. Because a Latin and Greek word sound alike we are tempted to think them allied, whereas resemblance of sound is a reason for regarding the words as from different roots. We take it for granted that the Spanish *mucho* and our *much* are the same, whereas there is no connection between them, nor is there any between the Greek ὅλος and our word *whole*. Dr. Johnson in his dictionary gave *curmudgeon* as derived from the French *cœur mechant*, a wicked heart. In reality it comes from *corn-mudgin*, one who stores up grain to create an artificial scarcity.*

A *salt-cellar* is referred to as if it were a cell in which to hold salt. The word *cellar* is originally *salarius*, a salt-holder, and has nothing to do with *cell*, which is connected with *celare*, to conceal.

The expression *stone-blind* means either blind as a stone, or else refers to the stony look, as of a white pebble, in the eyes of those afflicted with a certain form of blindness. Having this expression, we have manufactured another, *sand-blind*, out of semi-blind, to express near-sightedness. Because sand is finer than stones, men jumped at the conclusion that the proper expression for a degree less than stone-blindness would be "sand-

---

* Dr. Johnson gave "curmudgeon" as from *cœur* and *mechant*, and added the words "unknown correspondent," referring to his authority. Ashe, copying from Johnson, makes another more ludicrous mistake. He wrote: "Curmudgeon from *cœur*, unknown, and *mechant*, correspondent."

blind." Launcelot, in the "Merchant of Venice," goes on to divide the scale again by inventing the term *gravel-blind.**

Pliny actually thought that the *panther* was so called from παν φεριον, as if the animal combined the elements of all wild beasts—was an epitome of savage life; and another writer says the Latin *apis* is derived from the Greek ἄπους, footless, because at one stage of their existence bees are footless grubs.

In his powerful poem, "Childe Roland," Browning uses the expression *slug-horn:*

"I put the *slug-horn* to my lips and blew."

Slug-horn has a fine flavor of the Dark Ages, and suggests a connection with slug and slaughter, as if it meant a battle-horn. But its origin lies in a mistake of Chatterton's as to the meaning of the Celtic *slogan*, sometimes written *sloggorne*. So he wrote, "some caught a *slug-horn* and an onset wound," under the impression that a *sloggorne* was a musical instrument and not a battle-cry. Browning took from him the word "slug-horn," which is so expressive that it is a pity there is not something real to base it on.

---

* *Launcelot.* "This is my true-begotten father, who being more than sand-blind, high gravel-blind, knows me not."
—" Merchant of Venice," Act II., Scene ii., line 30.

Some one says that *legend* is derived from *lügende*, lying, because a legend has often so slight a foundation. Legends are *legenda*, tales of the martyrs or saints, read in the churches, "written with a purpose." So untrustworthy were they that legend has now come to mean a tale purporting to be history, but evidently not founded on fact. A tradition, on the other hand—meaning originally some statement handed down orally from father to son — is regarded as having probably a nucleus of truth. Legends are frequently invented to account for geographical names, and frequently based on some etymological mistake.

Thus, there is a mountain in Switzerland called Pilate's Mount, and a legend has been invented to account for the name. There is a small lake near the summit, and it is said that Pontius Pilate committed suicide by drowning himself in it, impelled by remorse for his part in the Crucifixion. In reality, the name—*Mons Pilatus*, or the hatted hill—comes from the fact that the summit is frequently surrounded by clouds, a phenomenon which has given a name to many mountains.

Sometimes the legend is invented, as in the above case, to fit the name, and sometimes the name is given to suit the legend. The most common error, however, is the warping of the spelling or pronunciation of a foreign name to render it similar to some word in the vernacular. Attention has already been called to the curious corruptions of some French geographical names in our country. Many other instances could be given. The mountain near the head of the bay of Fundy, called *Chapeau Dieu*, from the cap of cloud which often overhangs it, is now known as the *Shepody* Mountain. In England, "*Chateau Vert* has become *Shotover*, *Beau Chef*, *Beechy*, and *Burg Walter*, the castle of Walter of Douay, who came over with William the Conqueror, now appears in the form of *Bridgewater*. *Leighton beau désert* has been changed into *Leighton Buzzard*, and the brazen eagle which forms the lecturn in the parish church is exhibited by the sexton as the original buzzard from which the place derived its name." *Cape Horn* we naturally suppose to be so called because it is the end or horn of the Continent, whereas it is named from its discoverer.

In England the yeomen of the household guard are called *beef-eaters*. The derivation of this word is probably what the spelling indicates—at least there is no evidence to the contrary. With an excess of ingenuity, the etymologists of the last generation conjectured the origin to be *buffetier*, or waiter at a *buffet*, a sideboard. The derivation of the American expression "I don't care a *hooter*" from "don't care an *iota*" is so plausible that it would be a pity to have it disproved. Instances of the corruption of words by a popular desire to express the etymology are : *sparrow-grass* for *asparagus*, *court-cards* for *coat-cards*, *shuttlecock* for *shuttlecork*, *maul-stick* for *mahlerstuck*, *crayfish* for *écrevisse*, *dormouse* for *dormeuse*, *dandelion* for *dent de lion*, *country-dance* for *contredanse*. In *Webster's Unabridged*, *haberdasher* was said to come from the German, "*Habt Ihr dass, Herr?*" The English sailors called the ship *Bellerophon* "Bully Ruffian," and the *Hirondelle* the "Iron Devil;" and the English mob called *Ibrahim Pasha* "Abraham Parker." It will be seen that the professionals are sometimes as ingenious as the uninstructed.

In Scott's novel of *The Pirate*, Norna lived on the *Fitful Head*—a not inappropriate name. It comes from the old Norse name *Huit Fell*, or white headland. *Cunning Garth*, in Westmoreland, was originally the King's (Koening's) Yard. A widely-spread etymological error was the notion that *King* was originally *Kenning*, the man who knows, or, as Carlyle puts it, "the man who is able—who can." In reality the *ing* is the Saxon patronymic suffix. *Koening* is the son of the kin or tribe. *Devil* was once supposed to be from *do evil*. The name *God*, by a natural moral impulse, was supposed to be connected with the same root as *good*, though a little reflection would have made the etymology suspected, for God is a very old Teutonic word, and certainly antedates Christianity by many centuries. But an ante-Christian conception of deity never refers to the attribute of goodness. On the contrary, savage tribes are impressed with the idea of a being of irresponsible power, and therefore the root of the word *God* means that which can be propitiated. If the Teutonic race, or any other, could have worked out by themselves the belief in universal goodness, here would have been little need of a revelation.

The Greeks called Jerusalem *Hierosolyma*, as if it were the sacred city of Solomon. It is said that the name *Tatars* was in the thirteenth century changed into *Tartars*, to carry the idea that the hordes, whose invasion was thought to be a fulfilment of the prediction of the opening of hell, were direct from Tartarus. The tower of Saint Verena, near Grenoble, is called *Le Tour Sans Venin*, and to fit the name the peasantry have originated the superstition that no poisonous animal can live near it. In New York there is a square called "Grammercy Park," a name which might readily be supposed to be of French origin. But on an old map the locality is marked as occupied by a pond called *De Kromme Zee*, the crooked pond. *Equipage* has nothing to do with *equus*, a horse, but is from *equip*, to furnish. *Hessians* are not the boots worn by Hessians, but the word is probably connected with *hose*, since the shoe and the leg-covering are united. *Hangnail* is a nail that gives pain, or *anguish*, not one that hangs loose. *Gingerly* does not refer to ginger, but is from an old English root. *Incentive* is not that which incenses or causes to burn, but comes from *incantare*, to excite by singing, and is allied to incantations.

Mr. Taylor calls attention to the insistence with which Teutonic nations try to twist old Celtic local names into a form in which they would be susceptible of explanation from their own languages. The Celtic words *alt maen* mean high rock. In the Lake District this name has been transformed into the "*Old Man* of Coniston." In the Orkneys a peak or dome fifteen hundred feet high is called the "*Old Man* of Hoy." *The Dead Man*, another Cornish headland, is a corruption of the Celtic *dod mean*. *Brown Willy*, a Cornish mountain ridge, is a corruption of *Bryn Huel*, the tin-mine ridge. *Abermaw*, the mouth of the Maw, has become *Barmouth*.

Maidenhead was originally *Mayden hithe*, the "wharf midway" between Marlow and Windsor. From this name arose the myth that the head of one of the eleven thousand virgins of Cologne was buried here. Again, *Maidstone* and *Magdeburg* are not the maiden towns, but one is the town on the Medway, and the other the town of the plain. *Anse de Cousins*, the Musquito's bay, has been transformed by English sailors into

Nancy Cousin's bay. *Hagenes*, the Norse name of one of the Scilly isles, has become *St. Agnes*, and *Horace's Mountain* of Soracte is added to the list of saints by the Italian peasantry as *St. Oreste.* In New Brunswick, the river *Quah-Tah-Wah-Am-Quah-Duavic*, probably the most unmanageable name in the Gazeteer, has been abbreviated into the *Petam Kediac*, and transformed by the lumber men into *Tom Kedgwick.* In nearly every locality are to be found Indian names thus changed. No doubt *Tombigby* is an instance, and there was once a tendency to call Appalachian, *Apple-acorn.*

The following extract from the *Critic* will show, however, that it is not always the unlearned who invent words:

"An amusing illustration of the mechanical way in which dictionaries have been made, is furnished by the word *phantomnation*, which appears in *Webster*, *Worcester*, the *Imperial*, and *Cassell's Encyclopedic Dictionary*. *Webster* solemnly defines it thus: 'Phantomnation *n.* Appearance as of a phantom; illusion. [*Obs. and rare.*] *Pope.*' *Worcester* says simply: 'Illusion. *Pope.*' The *Imperial* and *Cassell's* repeat this bit of lexicographic wisdom; but the latter omits the reference to Pope, apparently suspecting that something is the matter somewhere. Now the source of this word is a book, entitled *Philology on the English Language*, published in 1820, by Richard Paul Jodrell, as a sort of supplement to *Johnson's Dictionary*. Jodrell had a curious way of writing phrases as single words, without even a hyphen to indicate their composite character; thus, under his wonder-working pen, *city solicitor* became 'citysolicitor,' *home acquaintance* 'homeacquaintance'—and so on indefinitely. He remarks in his preface that it 'was necessary to enact laws for myself,' and he appears to have done so with great vigor. Of course he followed his 'law' when he transcribed the following passage from Pope:

> These solemn vows and holy offerings paid
> To all the *phantom nations* of the dead.
> *Odyssey*, x., 627.

Phantom nations became 'phantomnations,' and the 'great standards of the English language' were enriched with a 'new word!' There is a difference, however, between Jodrell and his followers: *he* knew what Pope meant. *Webster's* definition is entirely original. This appears to have been the best instance of a 'ghost-word' on record."

Upstart, the name applied to a person whose antecedents do not justify his pretensions, is given in *Webster's Unabridged* as from *up* and *start*. The verb undoubtedly has this derivation, but the noun is from *up* and *start*, or *steort*, a tail, the same word which appears in the name of the bird, *redstart*, and in *stark-naked*. *Acorn* was very naturally supposed to be *oak-corn;* but Mr. Skeat shows that it meant originally wild fruit, and is based on *acker*, a field—cognate with Latin *ager*. Therefore, Chaucer was right and not tautological when he wrote, "acornes of okes."

Andiron is another word in which a false idea of the etymology has changed the spelling. Its real etymology is obscure, but it has nothing to do with iron. But there was a term in Saxon— *Brand-iron*—having nearly the same meaning, with which the old word *anderne* became confused.

Apace is used very early to signify rapidly.

Gallop *apace*, ye fiery-footed steeds.—*Marlowe*.

But it meant in Chaucer's time, slowly. He writes it *a pas*, signifying at a walk.

Còndign is now applied to punishment alone, but originally had the meaning of merited, *condignus*, in a general way, so that it was proper to say, "a condign reward" as well as "a condign punishment." This is, however, not an instance of an erroneous etymology, but of a limitation of the original meaning of a word.

Sirloin is a well-known instance of an erroneous etymology, detected many years ago. It was once said that Henry VIII. knighted jestingly a noble loin of beef. It is really *sur*, or *supra*, loin.

Surly was supposed to be *sourly*, but the early

spelling makes it highly probable that it is from *sir-like*, having the meaning *imperious*, from which the transition to its present force is easy enough. It would thus be analogous to *lordly*, which has retained the original meaning of arrogant bearing.

Dog-cheap is an odd word, when we think of it. It was explained by saying that dog's-meat was of a poorer quality, but so is that of cats and other carnivorous animals. There is a Swedish dialect word, *dog*, meaning *very*, and this dog in *dog-cheap* is probably the same word, though *cheap* is not Scandinavian. *Cheap*, meaning to buy, is a very old word in English, though probably of Latin origin. *Dog-cheap*, then, is very cheap.

The word *cock* illustrates as well as any other the many sources from which English has sprung: First, is *cock*, the male bird, from Latin through French, and from this comes the use of turn-*cock*, on account of some fancied resemblance to the tail of the fowl; second, a *cock* of hay is Scandinavian; third, "to *cock* one's eye," or a *cocked* hat, is Celtic; fourth, the *cock* of a gun is Italian, meaning the notch of an arrow, and probably the retaining notch on a cross-bow. The Germans have, by a natural etymological confusion, translated this *cock* by *hahn*—"*den hahn spannen*," to cock the gun; fifth, *cock*, in the sense of a small boat, as used in "Lear," and as compounded in *cockswain*, is a widely-spread word, also from Latin through French, but not connected with the first word, though from the same source.

Wormwood is given in *Webster*** as taking its name from the fact that its bitter taste made it fatal to worms. The old spelling, *wermode*, shows that this is not the derivation. It was then conjectured that it meant *ware-moth*, something that drives off insects. This hypothesis was found to be equally untenable, and Mr. Skeat conjectures that the original meaning was *ware-moad*, or mind-preserver, from the "supposed curative properties of the plant in mental affections," which is at least equally ingenious and much more probable.

The above examples will suffice to show that etymology is full of blind alleys, and that the only safe method is the scientific one, of: First, gathering facts patiently; secondly, classifying the facts till a general principle can be enunciated; and, thirdly, using this general principle with great care in examining the residual facts which are not readily explainable by the theory, but never forcing the facts into the theory.

* *Webster* here means the *Unabridged*. All the errors are corrected in the *International*, or last edition of *Webster*.

CHAPTER XIII.

ODD AND DISGUISED DERIVATIONS.

THE changes of pronunciation to which words are subject are never abrupt. If they were so the word would lose its identity. The phonetic law governing the change works very slowly, though much more rapidly at some periods than at others; but the result is a gradual change, a growth, and the operation is largely an unconscious one. Spelling, on the other hand, is artificial, and since the invention of printing has developed very little. Originally it was largely phonetic, and in some instances great pains were taken to make the letters represent the sound of the words as pronounced at the time. Our modern spelling is traditionary and made up of "unconsidered remnants." It is entirely arbitrary, and must always remain so, because a group of letters must represent a word, and a word is not a definite sound but a changing sound. Early spelling, however, indicates early pronunciation, or at least comparative pronunciation, which is the most that we can hope to arrive at in reading an unspoken or obsolete tongue. It is altogether improbable that Chaucer or Shakspeare could understand their own works as read by a modern, especially by one who aims to reproduce the ancient pronunciation. Nevertheless, we can say quite confidently that a certain combination of letters represented a definite sound in a thirteenth century book—in the *Ormulum* (A.D. 1215), for instance, which is a great deal more than we can say of any modern book, although it may be impossible to reproduce the sound vocally. It is evident, then, that early spelling is very useful—indeed indispensable—in tracing the pedigree of words. Sometimes a single, apparently superfluous, letter in a modern word betrays its origin. Letters as the indications of ancient pronunciation are the main guides in seeking for derivatives.

The value for etymological research of the silent, useless, and arbitrarily sounded letters in English words is, of course, no argument against phonetic spelling, and certainly none against such a moderate reform as would greatly lessen the number of letters we are forced to write, and subject English orthography to at least the outline of a system. The words in their antique garments would remain embalmed in old books and dictionaries for the use of philologists. A spelling reform is impossible for another reason.

ODD AND DISGUISED DERIVATIONS. 157

Printers and proof-readers will never permit it to be brought about. They have been forced to learn a certain system before they could obtain employment and cannot now learn another. Any modification of our present absurd system of spelling English words is hopeless, however desirable, on account of the practical difficulty of initiating changes in the memories of a great body of adults. If it could be made fashionable to spell lawlessly the first step would be taken, for then perhaps a coherent system might grow out of the ruins of the old one.

The changes in meaning through which a word sometimes passes in succeeding generations, though nearly always logical, are sometimes very complex. Consequently, if a link of the historical sequence is lost it is dangerous to attempt to supply it by conjecture. An abstract word grows out of a concrete word because we learn by experience to know concrete things first. But sometimes the meaning is boldly transferred in the other direction by an exercise of the radical metaphor-building faculty. The word is compounded with other words, and one of the words becomes an inseparable prefix or suffix, modifying the pronunciation or moving the accent. These changes, too, are growths, but sometimes they are very rapid, especially so during the formative period of the language. They take place, too, largely in the oral language and may not be recorded. Usually every step of the changes in meaning can be readily explained if it can be uncovered. But the range of the metaphorical word-building power is very great, and it works on individual words. Its results are, therefore, much more difficult to follow than are those of the sound-changing power, which works in uniform lines on great bodies of words and within physical limits.

These points, especially the last, explain why some derivations seem odd or unaccountable. Some of the words mentioned in the last chapter are illustrations of this, but there are others in which the connection between origin and meaning is even less obvious. How comes it that the word *frank*, which probably meant a javelin, should now mean outspoken? The Franks of history were originally a body of High Germans —a colonizing army rather than a tribe—and one of their arms was a spear. They called themselves spearmen or Franks. The territory they conquered came to be known as France. The members of the dominant people retained as the inheritance of conquerors certain civic privileges or immunities from civic burdens. It is easy to see how *Frank-rights* became the origin of franchise, and as a member of the ruling race can safely speak his mind, how *frank* came to mean outspoken.

Free is a word of ancient Teutonic root, meaning not restrained by formal rule. It has had two meanings simultaneously: courtesy and liberty. Chaucer says of the Knight:

> " He loved chivalrie,
> Trouth and honour, *freedom* and curte'sie."

Here, in an example of bilingualism, *freedom* is employed in the sense of gentlemanly manners resulting from a sense of not being constrained, and therefore natural and genial. Shakspeare also writes:

> "I thank thee, Hector:
> Thou art too gentle, and too *free* a man."

The meaning is evidently lordly, noble, gentle. This meaning is retained in the poetic phrase "fair and free," and in the common expression "free and easy," in which last case it is somewhat degenerated.

Barbour, a Scottish contemporary of Chaucer, writes:

> "*Freedom* is a noble thing;
> *Freedom* makes man to have liking,"

and contrasts freedom and thirldom, or thraldom. Here we have the meaning of civil liberty as opposed to slavery, in which sense the word is used to-day. Why do we call a tale, in inventing which the imagination is allowed free play, a *Romance*, after the most practical-minded race of history, instead of after the Greeks or the Arabs, people of far more poetic power? The reason is that Romans, or the Roman language, meant very early the popular tongue of France, as distinguished from the Latin of books. In this popular tongue tales were written, so that a *romaunt* became the name for a certain style of poem or tale, as the "*Romance* of Richard Cœur de Lion," and the "*Romaunt* of the Rose." The extravagance of these tales *in Romance* was so marked that the term was extended in time to cover any unbridled exercise of the imagination.

The connection between *candidate* and *candid*, or white, is not at once evident. It arose from the Roman fashion which dictated that those who presented themselves for election should signify their readiness by wearing white gowns. *Ambition* is derived from the practice of going about (*ambire*) to solicit votes. *Antic* is derived from ancient, or more properly from antique, ancient being of course the Romance form of the Latin *antiquus*. Anything old-fashioned is odd. Anything odd is meaningless. Then, by one of the inexplicable whims of word-appropriation *antic* was restricted to meaningless capers.

The *humanities* as applied to study now means the liberal branches. Originally it was used in distinction to theology, the one being regarded as human wisdom, the other as divine.

Trivial is supposed to be derived from *tres vias*, where three roads cross, therefore common, that which may be picked up anywhere; as we say of a sharp fellow who has not much depth, "he has been educated on the streets." Yet schools which taught grammar, arithmetic, and geometry were called *trivial* schools, or three-branch schools.

Insult originally meant to jump on a man (*insulto*), having previously knocked him down, "adding insult to injury;" but *affront* is to defy him to his face (*ad frontare*). "Proud Cumberland prances *insulting* the slain," is etymologically correct. We are very apt to confound this word with insolent (*in solens*), which means out of the common, and applies to indecorous conduct from one inferior in age or station.

Surround is a word having a strange history. It is *sur* (*supra*) and *unda*, a wave, and meant to cover with water: "As streams if stopt, *surrownd*," in Warner's *Albion's England* (*circ.* 1600). The word is not found in Shakspeare at all, for he uses *round* in the sense of encompass: "Our little life is *rounded* with a sleep." Nor does it appear in the Bible or Prayer-book. It was confused with *round* in the seventeenth century, and stole its meaning entirely, except in the usage of herdsmen, and now means to encompass, not to inundate. This word bases itself entirely on false pretences, but is firmly established in good standing.

Tarpaulin might more properly be noticed under hybrid words, for *tar* is a good old English word, and *pawling* is from the Latin *pallium*, a cloak or mantle, which gives also the word *pall*, a covering for the dead.

Nice, originally *nescius* (no science), ignorant, or unskilful, has passed through a variety of meanings, from ignorant to discriminating or exact, which is the proper use now, as "a *nice* observation," "a *nice* distinction," etc. *Nice*, in the sense of fitting, agreeable, is colloquial, and evidently derived from the idea of exactness. The connection between exactness and ignorance is not so evident, and the transference of meaning may probably have been influenced by the old English word *nesh*, which meant "delicate" as well as soft. Mr. Earle gives the following account of the gradual change of meaning: "The word dates from the great French period, and at first meant 'foolish, absurd, ridiculous;' then in course of time it came to signify 'whimsical, fantastic, wanton, adroit;' thence it slid into the meaning of subtle, delicate, sensitive, which landed it on the threshold of its modern meaning." Its use in social slang is too unscientific to be traceable. Indeed, the change of meaning is abnormal, at best.

Quaint is another word which has passed

through various vicissitudes of meaning. It is derived from the Latin *cognitus*, known, and in point of derivation is the same word as noble. It now means old-fashioned with a slight implication of simplicity and dignity. Professor Earle says: "We may almost say that the word *quaint* now signifies 'after the fashion of the seventeenth century.' It means something that is pretty after some by-gone standard of prettiness." In the fourteenth century it was a "great social word, describing an indefinite sort of merit and approbation." Chaucer calls the spear of Achilles a "*quaint* spear," for it could both hurt and heal. Shakspeare makes Prospero say "My *quaint* Ariel," and in "Much Ado About Nothing" speaks of a "fine, *quaint*, graceful, and excellent fashion."

Policy as applied to a written instrument, an insurance policy, is a word of ancient lineage and quite distinct from *policy*, line of public conduct, which is from πόλις, a city. The first comes from πολύς, much, and πτύξ, a fold, and means a long register in many leaves. Why the meaning should be limited as it is, is not known.

Average is a modern word in its present sense. It was used as meaning a common ratio to a number of different quantities by Adam Smith, the economist (*circ.* 1820). Now we use it to signify a number such that the sum of the *plus* differences between it and a given set of numbers is equal to the sum of the *minus* differences. This, though mathematically distinct from the first meaning, is popularly the same thing. In feudal times the word meant a contribution towards carrying the lord's wheat; then it came to mean a freight charge, and lastly, a contribution towards the loss of goods which were sacrificed to save the rest of the ship's freight. This contribution was proportioned or *averaged* according to the value of each shipper's goods. From this to the sense of a mean—the modern sense—the transition is easy. Each step of the change of meaning is logical, though the entire change presents a seemingly irreconcilable divergence.

Belfry has nothing to do with bell, but was originally *bercfrit*, or watch-tower, and was applied to the movable tower on wheels used in the Middle Ages to attack a walled town. It now means a tower for bells. The change of meaning is due to the sound of the first syllable.

Dirge, a funeral chant, comes from *dirige*, guide. In the Latin service for the dead, one part began, "*Dirige domine vitam meam.*" *Dirige* was contracted into *dirge*, and extended into a general word for any musical expression of grief.

Postumous, meaning last, was first applied to a child born after the father's death, though it meant simply the last born. Then an *h* was thrust into the word, as if it meant after burial

ODD AND DISGUISED DERIVATIONS. 165

in the ground. Finally, the meaning was restricted to a child born after the father's death, or to a work published after the author's death.

Spend, splay, and *sport* are an odd group of words. They are all Latin, yet have a decided appearance of belonging to old English stock. *Spend* is *dispendere*, to weigh out; *splay* is *displicere*, to unfold; *sport* is *disportere*, to carry hither and thither. In all cases the first letters of "dis" have dropped out of sight, and the *s*, in accordance with a phonetic law, has survived. *Sport* and *spend* have superseded the old forms, but *splay* has secured a standing in *splay-footed* only, *display* stubbornly holding its place.

Allow is a verb with a double root, or, rather, there were originally two verbs, *allow* from *allaudare*, to praise, and *allow* from *allocare*, to place, to expend—hence, an *allowance*, or money given. The first meaning can be found in the Bible and in Shakspeare: "Ye *allow* the deeds of your fathers."—Luke xi., 48. The use of *allow* in the sense of praise is obsolete, yet as there is a connection between *approval* and permission, the first meaning has colored the modern usage.

Amazement, as confusion of mind from whatever cause, and not, as now, simply astonishment; *depart*, in the sense of separate ("till death us *depart*," corrupted in the marriage service into "do part"), and many other old usages can be found in the Prayer-book.

Ampersand, the arbitrary character for the word *and*, has an odd origin. In repeating the alphabet, children were taught to close by saying, " X, Y, Z, and, *per se*, and "—that is, "*and* by itself." This, shortened into *ampersand*, became the name of the character. The character itself grew out of the Latin *et*, which the scribes wrote in an ornamental fashion, curling backward the tail of the *t* in a flourish.

As Dean Trench points out, a potent cause of change of meaning in words is euphemism, or a desire to avoid the direct name of something disagreeable or obnoxious, by substituting some term with pleasanter associations. *Adventurer* meant originally a bold man with a "heart for any fate " which might *come* to him or to which he might *come*. He took the chances in a legitimate mercantile risk. But the word was applied to the half-merchants, half-pirates of the seventeenth century, instead of naming them honestly after their profession. Since then *adventurer* has come to mean one who preys on society in a pretentious and dashing manner. Singularly enough, *adventurous* retains the primitive meaning of fearlessness based on self-reliance—readiness to meet danger half-way.

In much the same way a *gambler* meant originally a person who plays a game, but now is restricted to one who plays unfairly for money. We are continually inventing euphemisms for *drunk*, like intoxicated, overcome, and a multitude of other expressions, most of which carry the idea that the condition was an accident, and not the result of weakness of the will. Nor do we hesitate to palliate breaches of the sexual obligation by some word or paraphrase which implies an excuse.

Again, *party-spirit*, the desire to cast contempt or opprobrium upon opponents, operates to change the force of words. *Whig* and *Tory* were originally nicknames. *Quaker*, *Puritan*, *Malignant*, *Methodist*, *Roundhead*, were names given by opponents. *Prime-minister*, or *Premier*, was a title sarcastically given to Walpole. These, however, have all remained names, and have not, with the possible exception of *premier*, which designates the functions of a member of the English Ministry, become real words.

Pigeon English is said to be " business English " —that is, a jargon invented for the purposes of trade with savages.

Business, Skeat gives as from the English adjective *busy*, but Earle thought that there was no connection between them, and that *business* was from the French word *besogne*, as seen in the modern French, *Faites votre besogne* ("do your duty"). As this is so much less simple than the other, it is not to be preferred without good evidence from ancient usage, which has not been found.

Canter, the slow gallop of a horse, is derived from Canterbury. The connection is, that the pilgrims to Canterbury were accustomed to make their horses take that gait. This is a very odd derivation, but that it is the true one is evident from early use. One of the latest examples is from Dr. Johnson: "The Pegasus of Pope, like a Kentish post-horse, is always on the *Canterbury*."

Calipers, the instrument for measuring the diameter of a cylinder, was first "*caliper* compasses." *Caliper* is the same as *caliber*, which is from a French word, *qualibre*, meaning quality or rank. Of this last the derivation is uncertain.

The forces which affect the significance of words, and color the exact shade of meaning they convey, are numberless. They cover all human mental activity. Some words become more dignified, their meanings grow fuller and more elevated; others sink and become degraded by association till they lose standing entirely. *Paramour, ringleader, traducer, dunce, equivocate, imp, gloze, silly, simple, prude*, and many others, had once nothing derogatory in their signification. *Sacrament, Christian, eucharist, humility, martyrs, regeneration*, have been elevated by Christianity. In fact, words record all the great movements of thought, the changes in character that distinguish different ages of the world. Sometimes language is affected and precise, sometimes free and strong. The causes of growth or loss of meaning are too broad and general to be classified. In fact, every word is a text for a chapter, if its various senses be collated and the reasons for the changes sought. An abstract word is but a form for an idea, and concrete words are not much more. As thought is in a perpetual flux, so must the forms of thought be also. The following are suggested as illustrations: *Knave, villain, boor, varlet, valet, menial, minion, pedant, swindler, timeserver, conceit, carp, officious, demure, crafty, artful, tinsel, specious, voluble, plausible, lewd, animosity, prejudice, askance, fulsome, gaudy, gush, hypocrite, monster, sad, zealot, brave, prude.*

Two instructive modern books on the growth of the English language are *Modern English*, by Fitzedward Hall, and *Standard English*, by F. L. Kington Oliphant.

CHAPTER XIV.

GEOGRAPHICAL NAMES.

LOCAL names of the great features of the earth —seas, rivers, lakes, mountains, and islands—are not arbitrary sounds; they were originally given with a purpose, and are frequently of great antiquity. Local names of civil divisions—counties, towns, hamlets, even fields—often embody a great deal of history. These names, too, gather associations, and their interest depends greatly on these associations. A knowledge of the derivations frequently widens very greatly these associations or connected ideas, for the history of the successive races that have occupied the land is impressed on the names of their old homes. Our country is unfortunate in this respect. We have, it is true, preserved many—too few—of the Indian names of lakes, rivers, and mountains; but the American aborigines are not, like the Celts and the Teutons, ancestors of modern civilization. Seneca, Cayuga, Niagara, Ontario, are fine words, and it is well that they have not been lost. It was a sad confession of intellectual poverty to name the townships of Western New York after the cities or heroes of classical antiquity—Marcellus, Rome, Pompey, Syracuse, etc., and it will be many years before the incongruity ceases to be full of absurd suggestions. Nor are the names of the Presidential range—Mount Washington, Jefferson, etc.—to be commended. Even the cacophonous Indian names of Maine are better than these, because they are not artificial. A more modern instance of the same bad taste is the attaching the names of the Queen of England and her husband and son to the great lakes of Africa. A civil geographical division may take the name of its founder, and there is reason in giving the name of the discoverer even to some great natural feature of the earth. No one would wish to change the name of Hudson's or of Baffin's Bay, because these words are the records of perseverance and courage. The value of the associations in a name which connects the present with the past is greater than is supposed. It is a continual suggestion of poetry. Otherwise we might as well adopt numbers at once, which, indeed, as in the streets of new cities, is a convenient method of ticketing localities which have no history and no individuality and no distinction.

Nevertheless, many local names in our country, though not relating to a distant past, have considerable historical interest. The rule that names of rivers are permanent is exemplified by the fact that all of our important rivers have retained their Indian names, except the St. Lawrence and the Hudson. The gulf into which the former of the two rivers flows, was discovered on the day sacred to St. Lawrence, and the gulf narrows by degrees into the river. In the same way the Hudson has in its lower course the character of an arm of the sea, and lacks the life and individuality of a river.*

The civil names on the map of North America testify to the original colonization by English, French, and Spaniards; and the lines which marked the territory originally occupied by each can be approximately determined by the character of the old names. Thus, France held possession of the valley of the Mississippi; and Louisiana, New Orleans, St. Louis, St. Charles, Detroit—the narrow strait—still witness to the French occupation. The names of the Jesuit missionaries, Père Marquette, Allouez, and Joliet, give a slight flavor of the seventeenth century to towns which have grown up in the country where their missions were established. Lake Champlain takes its name

---

* In South America the Spaniards disregarded the real names of the rivers in many cases, as La Plata, Amazon, San Francisco, Madeira, etc. The Amazon was discovered by Orellana, who said that a race of female warriors existed on its banks. The name is therefore a double fraud.

from the bold Norman adventurer who, "delighting marvellously in such enterprises," joined an Indian war-party and explored the upper waters of the St. Lawrence. The name of the State of Vermont shows that it came within the French dominion. *Fort Du Quesne*, the key to the Valley of the Ohio, became Pittsburg, in honor of the great war-minister under whom the empire of the New World was wrested from France.

When one race settles in a country occupied by a foreign population, it frequently modifies in imitation of the words of its own speech the local names of the country. Thus in Newfoundland— now belonging to the English, but a country where the French had fishing settlements—many of the bays and capes bear the old French names, ludicrously corrupted into vulgar English. For instance, *Rencontre* is changed into *Round Counter;* *Baie de Lièvre* is *Bay Deliver*, and *Baie des Espoirs* has become the *Bay of Despair*. In Michigan, too, the island *Bois Blanc* is written *Boblo*, *L'Isle Aigailée* is the original of the well-known lighthouse *Skilagalee*, and the *Sault Ste. Marie* is habitually spoken of and even written as the *Soo*. The name *Purgatoire* is corrupted into *Picketwire* River, and *Prairie des Perdrix* is said to be the original of *Dippertree Prairie*.

The Spanish names on the Pacific Coast are usually taken from the names of saints. Here the Spanish names again contradict the rule that the "rivers and mountains receive their names from the earliest races, villages and towns from later colonists." They called the rivers Colorado or Sacramento or Del Norte with a haughty indifference to their real names. As the occupation of the United States took place after the general diffusion of printing, the spelling of the Spanish names remains unchanged, though the pronunciation is often ludicrously corrupted; and it remains a disputed point—which will soon settle itself—whether or not (and, if at all, how far) to anglicize the Spanish pronunciation. Thus *Santa Fé* and *San Diego* are pronounced as they are written and with the *a* as in Samuel. *Sierra* and *Nevada* retain the Spanish vowel-sound. However pronounced, these names are memorials, in the early history of the extreme West, of the attempt of a moribund civilization to rejuvenate itself, and are in every respect superior to those of modern manufacture, which embody either a lamentable attempt at poetry or some commonplace reminiscence of early mining camps. About the Spanish names lingers a romance and a flavor of the past, in a country where romance and a past are sadly needed.

In our country some names have been manufactured. *Pomfret* is derived from *Pontefract*. A very odd name of a village in one of our Western

GEOGRAPHICAL NAMES. 175

States is *Yreka*, which the future etymologist will no doubt explain as a corruption of *Eureka*. In reality, it was suggested by the sign of a bakery, which, printed in large letters on a window-curtain, was legible from the inside, but from the outside appeared reversed, with the initial "B" concealed behind the right-hand casing. This must rank as the most singular origin of a geographical name on record. Our Connecticut ancestors made up some town names by an entirely original method. When wild land that lay between two towns, or was claimed as common land by two or more of the old towns, was set off as the abode of a new community, the name was made by amalgamating syllables from the names of the old towns. Thus *Harwinton* is *Har*tford-*Win*dsor *town; Winton-bury* is *Win*dsor-Farming*ton*-Sims*bury; Stratfield*, the old name of Bridgeport, is *Strat*ford-Fair*field; Stamwich* is *Stam*ford-Green*wich;* and *Hadlyme* is *Had*ley-*Lyme*. There is a self-conscious ingenuity about this method which forbids our recognizing it as a genuine folk-name formative process.

The names in the English settlements embody certain facts of early history. Passing over the Indian names which have survived, we note that the local names in New England, New York, and Virginia are colored by the characteristics of the settlers. Plymouth, Boston, Worcester, Cambridge,

Hartford, remind us of the parts of England from which the Puritans emigrated, and Salem was intended to be an "earthly realization of the New Jerusalem" which Calvinism was to inaugurate. We find very few references to the aristocratic forms of the country which they left. That Virginia—named from Queen Elizabeth, the Virgin Queen—was settled by loyal subjects of the King of England, is evident as we enter Chesapeake Bay. The river near the mouth is the James, so called in honor of the sovereign, and on either side are Capes Henry and Charles, bearing the names of his two sons, the hopeful prince whose succession to the throne might have changed the entire course of English history, and his unfortunate brother who became Charles I. Elizabeth County is named from their sister, the mother of Prince Rupert. The State of Delaware was founded in 1610 by Lord De la Warr, and Maryland commemorates Henrietta Maria, the Queen of Charles I. Baltimore is the Celtic name of a village in Ireland, from which Lord Baltimore derived his title. The city of Charleston, Albemarle Sound, the rivers Ashley and Cooper, and the States of North and South Carolina refer plainly in their names to the Restoration and the worthless Charles II. Annapolis is named from Queen Anne; Georgia, the youngest of the original thirteen States, from George II.; Fredricksburg from his son. These names indicate the original political character of the settlements and the contrast between them and New England. New York dates from the reign of Charles II., as it was granted to his brother, Duke of York and Albany. Its chief cities, New Amsterdam and Fort Orange, were rechristened, after the Dutch were dispossessed, New York and Albany. Some Dutch names survived—the Katskill Mountains, Fishkill, Staten Island, Brooklyn, Haarlem, Watervliet, Haverstraw, and others, to testify to its original colonization, but they are surrounded by English names. New Rochelle was settled by Huguenot refugees and named after their French home.

The history which is exemplified in the local nomenclature of our continent is comparatively recent. But the names of rivers, States, mountains, and cities in Europe belong in many instances to a remote past. The migrations of prehistoric races—Phœnicians, Celts, and Iberians—can be dimly traced on the modern map by names, which are the distorted survivals of those given two or three thousand years ago. The study of these linguistic relics has proved a valuable adjunct to ethnology, as the crushed and deformed relics of animal life have to paleontology. Nine-tenths of the geographical names of England are fossil-words containing some record of the life of forgotten tribes. This is a feature of interest which a new country like America can never possess. To give a few instances, the names of tribes are preserved, as of the Parisii in Paris, of the Dammonii in Devon, of the Boii in Bohemia; of ancient families, like that of the Æscings, the royal family of Kent, in Agincourt, France, and in Essington, Staffordshire; of individuals, as Marlborough, Merlin's barrow, or hill, in Hampshire; and of battles, boundaries, dwellings, temples, sacred places, camps, in profusion. We will confine ourselves to the consideration of a few points referring to some of the fuller treatises on this interesting branch of the study of words.*

Nations or tribes very frequently have two names, one by which they call themselves, and another by which they are known to foreign nations. The regular ethnic name frequently signifies the "speakers," or the "people," and the name given by other nations frequently means the foreigners, or the jabberers. Thus the people of England call themselves the English, while the Celtic peoples — the Welsh, the Manxmen, the Gaels of Scotland—call them *Saeson, Saoz, Sasunnaich,* or *Sagsonach.* The natives of Wales call

---

* Much of this chapter is taken from Taylor's *Names and Places.*

themselves *Cymry;* we call them *Welshmen.* The root of this word *Welsh* appears in a large number of ethnic names. All nations of Teutonic blood have called the bordering tribes by the name of *welchers*—that is, foreigners. *Waelschland* is the old German name of Italy. The Bernese Oberlander calls the French-speaking district to the south of him by the name of Canton-*Wallis*. *Wallenstadt* and *Wallensee,* the foreign city and the foreign lake, are on the frontier of the Romansch district. The Germans called the Bulgarians *Wallachi,* and their country *Wallachia,* and the Celts of Flanders were called *Walloons* by their Teutonic neighbors.

The roots *gal* and *wal* have frequently been confounded, and it is in some cases, no doubt, impossible to distinguish them. The Teutonic *w* and the Celtic and Romance *g* are convertible letters. The French *Gualtier* and *Guillaume* are the English Walter and William. So *guerre* and *war, gard* and *ward, guise* and *wise, guile* and *wile, guarantee* and *warranty,* are the same words. *Calais* was *Galeys* or *Waleys,* and the name no doubt indicates, whatever the root, the existence of a Celtic remnant surrounded by Teutonic settlers. The French to-day call the Prince of Wales "*le prince de Galles.*"

Gal, from *Gadhael* or *Gael,* is probably an independent Celtic root, for it was used as a national appellation by the Gaels of Ca*l*edonia,* Ga*l*way, Donne*gal*, Ga*l*loway, and Ar*gyle*, the Ga*l*atians to whom St. Paul wrote, and possibly by the inhabitants of Portu*gal*. *Gallia*, the word used by the Romans, is not connected with *Gael*, but may be from the root *wal*, the Teutonic appellation, *stranger*. This instance of the confusion between the Teutonic root *wal* and the Celtic root *gal* shows how much study as well as care and acuteness is necessary in the examination of derivations. It is beset with endless pitfalls for the unwary.

To return to the subject of double ethnic names. The Germans call themselves *Deutsche*, a word meaning the people; the French call them *Les Allemands*, from the name of the ancient frontier tribe, which probably means the other men or foreigners, outsiders.† The etymology of the word *German* is doubtful; possibly it comes from the Celtic *gairmean*, one who cries or yells in trying to talk. The Russians call the contiguous Ugrian tribes *Tschudes*, which means strangers. The Egyptians, and afterwards the Greeks, called

---

* This word is usually derived from *Coildooine*, the men of the woods. If it contains the root *Gal*, it would mean the Gaels of the dunes or hills.

† Orlando, in "As You Like It," when asserting his claim to social sympathy, says, "Yet am I *inland* bred." He uses *inland*, not as opposed to seaboard, but as opposed to *outland*, just as we use outlandish for grotesque or uncultured.

all who did not speak their own language *barbarians*, which may be traced to the Sanskrit root, *varvara*, one who speaks confusedly. The Greeks called themselves ethnically, *Hellenes*, but the Romans carelessly applied to them the name of the *Græci*, a small and unimportant tribe with whom they first came into contact, who were probably not Hellenes at all. This is but one of a number of misnomers, just as we carelessly use *Jew, Israelite,* and *Hebrew* indifferently. *Jew* is the name from the point of view of their religion, *Israelite* is the national name, and *Hebrew* is the ethnic or race name. But the distinctions are rarely observed in use, except by the most careful historians. A mediæval error is perpetuated whenever we speak of *Gypsies*, for the Gypsies did not come from Egypt, but probably from India, and they call themselves the Romany or else the Zincali—the last being the true name. Numerous other instances of this rule of double ethnic names might be gathered.

Another root which is frequently found in the names of peoples is *ar*. This ancient word, which is found in the vocabulary of all Indo-Germanic peoples, seems to have referred primarily to the occupation of agriculture.

Thus, in Greek, ἀρόω .... means to plough.
" " Latin, *aro* .... " "

Thus, in Gothic, *arjan*....... means to plough.
" " Polish, *orac*......... " "
" " old High German, *aran* " "
" " Irish, *araim*......... " "
" " old English, *ear*..... " "
" " Norse, *ard*......... " a plough.
" " English, *aroma* means odor of freshly-ploughed land.
" " English, *harrow* means to pulverize the surface.
" " Sanskrit, *arya* means a landholder, hence a member of the dominant race, a man as opposed to a slave. King Darius, a Persian, proudly claimed to be an "*Arya* of the *Aryans*."

The name of this Aryan race is to be found in the names *Iran*, *Herat*, *Aral*, *Armenia*, and possibly in *Iberia* and *Erin*. In languages of the Teutonic branch we find this root in the form *ware*, inhabitants. *Burhvare*, or burghers, are citizens of a burgh; *skipveri*, or shippers, are sailors. It is Latinized into the forms *vari*, *uari*, and *bari*, as the *Inguarii*, the *Ripuarii*, the *Chattuarii*, the *Ansibarii*, etc. The *Bulgarians* were the men from the Bolg or Volga, and *Boivarii* is preserved in the word *Bavaria*, while the home of the *Boii* has become *Bohemia*. In England *Worcester* is a corruption of *Hwic-wara-caster*, the camp of the men of the *Huiccii.* The men of Kent were *Cant-ware*, and their chief town is Cant-er-bury, the burgh of the men of Kent. This term survives in the Latin title of the archbishop, *Episcopus Cantuariensis*. *Carisbrooke*, in the Isle of Wight, was originally written *Gwiti-gara-burg*, the fort of the men of Wight. The first two syllables were dropped, and the *burg* became *bruk*, then *brooke*. The names *Cant* and *Gwiti* are still older Celtic words—that is, were geographical names before the archaic word *ware* (or *gara*) was added to them.

The syllable *set* is frequently found in the names of places. It means the seat or place inhabited by settlers, thus Somer-*set*, Dor-*set;* and *Alsace* is the other *set*, or the settlement west of the Rhine. *Holstein* is not the forest stone, but the forest settlement, *Holtsaetan*. These few instances may serve to show that a great deal of ancient history is embodied in words. The subject is a very broad one, and demands great care and patience.

The traces of the Roman occupation are found all over Europe in camps, roads, and in the Latinized forms of the ancient names of cities, especially of cities which from their situation had military importance in controlling the surrounding districts. The character of the Romans as strategists and intrusive administrators, not colonists, is as evident from the character of the local names derived from their language which have been incorporated into English, as from the remnants of their walls, military roads, villas, and camps which have survived through fifteen centuries.

We will close this brief reference to the subject of geographical names by calling attention to the fact that nearly all of the great rivers of Europe contain a Celtic root in their names. When a race enters a new country it is, of course, most likely to follow the river valleys, which afford the best land for settlement and the most convenient road for penetrating the wilderness. Hence a river is apt to have the same name for its entire course. The first-comers would naturally call the stream by a generic name, the *river*, or the *water*, or perhaps distinguish it by some adjective, as the *swift*, the *crooked*, the *sandy*, or the *big* river. Supposing that it was called simply the *water*. When the first settlers are dispossessed by an intrusive race, the new-comers, not being familiar with the language, would take the word *water* for a specific or proper name, and would add to it the word river in their own speech. This amalgamation is evident in the names of many rivers in England and on the Continent.

Almost all of the larger rivers of Europe contain one or more of the following Celtic roots for water or stream:

GEOGRAPHICAL NAMES. 185

1. *Avon* or *aon* or *awn*.
2. *Dwr* or *ter*.
3. *Uisge*, or *wysk, wye, is, es, oise, usk, esk, ex, ax*.
4. *Rhe* or *Rhin*, swift flowing.
5. *Don* or *Dan*.

Thus it seems probable that the name

Danaster or *Dniester*.....	contains roots	5, 3, 2
Rhadanau...............	" "	4, 5, 1
Rhodanus...............	" "	4, 5
Danubius...............	" "	5, 1
Rhenus.................	" "	4, 1
Eridanus................	" "	4, 5
Exter...................	" "	3, 2

We have the Stratford *Avon*, the Bristol *Avon*, and the Hampshire *Avon;* the *Ive* in Cumberland, the *Inn* in Fife, and the *Tyrol*, the *Auney*, the *Ewenny*, the *Wye*, the *Eveneny*, and the *Inney*—all from the first root. A great number of the names of French rivers end in *on, ome,* or *one*.

The syllable *Dur, Der, Stour,* forms part of innumerable river names, as the *Derwent*, the *Darwin*, the *Dart*—there are four river Derwents in England—and the *Adar*, the *Adder*, and the *Adur*.

The third root is in the *Esk*, in Scotland; the *Iz*, the *Isis*, and the *Thames* or the *Tamesis*, the broad *Isis*. The *Axe* and the *Ouse* are also the same word, and the root appears in innumerable combinations.

The fourth root, the *Rhe, Rhin,* or *Rhine* appears in the English streams the *Rye*, the *Ray*, the *Rhee*, the *Wrey*, the *Rhoe*, and several others.

The fifth appears very generally on the Continent and in the British Isles in the *Don*, the *Dane*, the *Dun*, the *Tone*, and the *Tyne*, *Teagn*, and *Teyn*. From the fact that the Celts named the rivers, the inference is irresistible that they were the first-comers, unless it can be shown that some of these roots were common to the speech of other races. That the English came later is evident from such words as Dur-*beck*, Is-*bourne*, Ash-*bourne*, Wash-*bourne*, Ouse-*burn*, where the Teutonic words *beck* and *burn*, or *brook*, have been added to the corruptions of the Celtic word for stream. In the name *Wans-beck-water* we find the Celtic *Wan* or *avon*, the *s* probably a remnant of *wysk*, the English *beck*, and the modern *water*. Thus we have the singular compound River-water-stream-water.

From the names of villages, fields, hills, woods, valleys, inferences may be drawn as to the distribution of the races from whom the modern inhabitants are descended. Mr. Taylor gives the following table:

PERCENTAGE OF NAMES FROM:	Suffolk.	Surrey.	Devon.	Cornwall.	Monmouth.	Isle of Man.	Ireland.
Celtic.......	2	8	32	80	76	59	80
Anglo-Saxon.	90	91	65	20	24	20	19
Norse.......	8	1	3	0	0	21	1

The derivations of the family names of any locality would, with certain modifications, yield evidence to the same point.

By far the greater part of the Celtic names in England are Cymric, but a thin stream of Gadhaelic names extends across the island from the Thames to the Mersey, as if to indicate the route by which the Gaels crossed and went to Ireland. From the North of Ireland the Gaelic tribe, the Scoti, crossed into Argyle, and in their turn partially dispossessed the Cymry of the Lowlands, who were probably the people known to history as the Picts. To determine the territory occupied by the Cymry and the Gaels, the words *Pen* and *Ben*— both meaning mountain—are useful test-words; also the words *inver* and *aber*, both meaning the mouth of a river, as *Inverness* and *Aberdeen*. In Ireland we find only *Invers*, but in Scotland *Invers* and *Abers*, both. *Bally*, a town, occurs 2000 times in Ireland and a few times in the Gaelic part of Scotland. If we draw a line from a point a little south of Inverary to a point a little south of Aberdeen, the *Invers* lie to the north-west of the line, and the *Abers* to the south-east of it, with few exceptions. The Celtic names in the Isle of Man are all Gaelic. There are ninety-six beginning with *Balla*, for instance. The names of the places connected with Christian worship are all Norse, indicating that here the Celts remained heathen, though Christianized on the mainland long before the Saxons or Danes. In the Channel Islands all the names of the towns and villages are derived from the names of saints, indicating that before the introduction of Christianity the islands were very sparsely populated, or, at least, that no towns were built.

To determine the settlement by Saxons or Danes the following syllables are test-words: For the Saxons, *ton, ham, worth, stoke, fold, yard, park, bury, barrow, ford;* for the Northmen, *by, thorpe, toft, ville, garth, ford* (or frith), *wick, ness, scar,* and *thwaite. Ton* means a place enclosed by a hedge—a family settlement—and is the origin of our word *town.* In some parts of England they still call the stack-yard the *barton,* or enclosure for what the land bears (or else the barley-yard), and in a few cases isolated farm-houses bear the name *ton,* as Shotting*ton,* Apple*ton,* and Wingle*ton.* The word *yard* had nearly the same original signification as *ton,* and the Norse equivalent *garth. Tine,* a twig—surviving in the tyne of a pitchfork—bears the same relation to *ton* and *town* that *yard,* a little stick—surviving in *yard-measure*—does to *yard,* an enclosure. *Stoke* means a place enclosed by stakes, and *fold,* an enclosure made by felled trees, or by felling the trees—a *field,* a clearing. *Worth* is a place warded or guarded. *Park* also meant an enclosed field, and a *hay* is a place surrounded by a hedge.

A very large number of towns and villages in England and Scotland—certainly not less than one thousand—have the termination *borough*, *bury*, *barrow*, and *burgh*, as Gains*borough*, Edin*burgh*, Salis*bury*, and *Barrow*-in-Furness. The original meaning of this terminal, Anglo-Saxon *burh* or *burg*, is earthwork, from a verb meaning to protect, *beorgan*. A funeral mound protects the body, and is called a *barrow*, whence the verbs to *bury* and to *burrow*. Since the fort or protected place would usually be an elevated ground, or would be surrounded by an artificial mound of earth, we have sometimes confounded the Anglo-Saxon termination *burgh* with the word meaning hill, which we have in ice*berg*. In Scotland the termination retains its original roughness, and is spelled *burgh*. In the north of England it is softened into *borough*, and in the south and west into *bury*. In many of the places in England ending in *borough* or *bury* the remains of the ancient hill-fort can be found near by, and, in some cases, it is known by the name of Castle, as *Marbury* Castle and *Wemsbury* Castle. In many cases this earthwork is of Celtic origin, though perhaps utilized by the Saxon conquerors, and given the Saxon name after it had been lost by the original builders. The one best worth visiting is the great mound at *Marlborough*, in Wilts, where is now one of the great modern schools. *Marlborough* is Merlin's barrow, and the tradition is that the mound is Merlin's grave. A part of London is called the *Borough*. This is named from an ancient earthwork which once protected the city on that side.

The suffix *ham* is distinctively Saxon. It is the same word as home. Thus we have Northam, Allingham, Buckingham, etc. Sometimes the *ham* is united to *ton*, as *Hampton*, *Southampton*, indicating, perhaps, that the home has developed into a ton or town. In very many cases the syllable *ing* is combined with *ton*. *Ing* is the patronymic or tribal designation. Thus the *Warings* are the tribe or family of *Waer*, and their settlement was *Warington*; and *Allingham* was the home of the tribe of *Al*; *Arlington* the ton of the children of *Arl*. This syllable *ing* is Saxon and Norse both. Thus the *Vaeringer*, or Norse soldiers employed by the Saracens were *Warings*. The syllables *ham* and *ton* and *ing* in the names of French towns, as *Aubinges*, *Beaubigny*, *Brantigny*, derived from settlements of the *Æbing*, the *Bobbing*, the *Branting*, determine the limits of the Saxon settlements in France, and, when found in German towns, indicate the original home of the Saxons and their allied tribes.

The Norse settlements are indicated by the syllable *by* or *bye*, a home, which in Normandy takes the form *bœuf* or *bue*. Thus, in the Danish district of England we find towns called *Grimsby, Derby, Whitby, Rugby, Kirby*.

Thorpe means a village, as in *Althorpe*, etc. *Toft*, or, in Normandy, *tot*, as in *Ivetot*, Ivo's *toft* or homestead, is Danish as distinguished from Norwegian; but *Thwaite*, a field, is Norwegian.

Ville, in many cases, is Romance from *villa*, but is also Norse, from *weiler*, a house. In England it is found sometimes as *well* or *will*, as in *Kettlewell*.

Ford, in both Saxon and Norse, is connected with the word *faran*, to go, which we see in *farewell* and *fare*, cost of travelling. But the Saxon *ford* is a place for passing a river for man and beasts, while the Norse *ford* is *fiord*, a navigable arm of the sea. Thus *Oxford* is the place to cross the river Ox, but *Wexford, Deptford,* and *Carlingford* are named from bays or creeks, and are Norse names.

Another Norse word which may be confounded with a similar Saxon one is *wic*. With the Norsemen it meant a harbor or bay, hence *Wikings* or *Vikings* are baymen, or longshoremen. *Sandwich* is Sandy bay, and *Berwick, Wicklow*, etc., names given to places near the sea, are Norse.

Ness or *Naze*, a nose or rocky promontory, and *scar*, a cliff, seen in *Caithness, Scarborough*, and the *Skerries*, indicate Norse occupation.

On comparing the Saxon and Norse geographical names* we note that the proportion of *tons* and *hams*, compared to *byes*, *thwaites*, *thorpes*, varies in different localities, and indicates the territories where each race settled. Again, the *tons* and *hams* indicate tribal settlements, for they are generally united to *ing*, but the *byes* are preceded by the name of an individual. Thus *Grimsby* is the place where Grim, a captain of a band of sea-rovers, settled with his men; but *Buckingham* is a tribal home, not named from one man. In both cases the fact of the detached character of the Teutonic settlements, referred to by Tacitus,† is well brought out, for all the Saxon syllables *ham*, *ton*, *yard*, etc., indicate an enclosed and guarded place. This love for a fenced-off, private ownership of land is still characteristic of Englishmen.

The study of the derivations of geographical names adds very greatly to the interest of travel, and gives reality to history. In particular, the

---

* The class of names resulting from the early Norse invasions must not be confounded with the much later Norman-French names in England.

† Nullas Germanorum populis urbes habitari satis notum est, ne pati quidem inter se junctas sedes. Colunt discreti ac diversi, ut fons, ut campus, ut nemus placuit. Vivos locant non in nostrum morem connexis et cohærentibus ædificiis; suam quisque domum spatio circumdat, sive adversus casus ignis remedium sive inscitia ædificandi. — TACITUS *Germania*, 16.

names of the streets, houses, and places in London embody, frequently in a very odd and striking way, a great many historical events. This is true of Cheapside, Pall Mall, Temple Bar, Piccadilly, High Holborn, Southwark, the Savoy, Rotten Row, and many other London names.

Besides Mr. Taylor's book, *Names and Places*, my acknowledgments to which have already been made, Edmunds's *Traces of History in the Names of Places* may also be read. *Webster's Unabridged* contained a list of geographical etymologies unfortunately omitted in the *International*. The popular etymologies of Indian names, as Alabama (here we rest), Kentucky (dark and bloody ground), etc., are usually pure inventions. Blakie's *Etymological Dictionary of Place Names* is useful for reference.

CHAPTER XV.

SURNAMES.

LOGICALLY, a proper name is a different kind of word from a common noun, for it is a word appropriated to a single individual. Strictly speaking, a proper name has no meaning, or at best but an arbitrary and temporary one. We call a man John, but the word is not exclusively appropriated to him, and does not convey the slightest information about him to a stranger. His surname indicates that his father bears the same last name, but affords no clew to the character of the man himself. But, philologically, surnames and Christian names do not differ from other words. They are growths, and every syllable of them has or once had a meaning. We confine ourselves to the consideration of surnames because they are comparatively modern in origin—not dating back beyond the tenth century. Given names, on the contrary, are of extreme antiquity. Harold and Albert and Edward and Edith were names borne by our Saxon ancestors before the Conquest;

John, Elias, Abraham, Noah, and Adam antedate English history itself.

The word *surname* is not, as might naturally be supposed, derived from *sire name*, or father name, but from *supra nomen*, or extra name. We know this because it is spelled with a *u*, and not with an *i*, and also from the fact that in the Provençal language it is written *soubrenom*. The question of early spelling is often of the greatest importance in tracing derivations. If it is possible to follow a family name back through old deeds, wills, tax-lists, court-records, etc., to the fourteenth century, the early spelling will almost invariably furnish a clew to the original meaning, for names were rarely given arbitrarily, but usually for some evident reason.

The old spelling will also frequently determine which of the possible derivations is the true one. Thus the name *Woodman* might originally mean a forester, or it might possibly once have been written *Woadman*, which means dyer, from *woad*, the native indigo used by both Britons and Saxons in dying the rough woollen cloth they made. *Coleman* might be a maker of charcoal for the forges of the primitive smiths, or it might be cunning man, since *col* meant cunning. This syllable *col* is seen in the name *Colfax*, or the cunning fox. The syllable *fax* might be originally fox, or it might come from *facere*, to do, as in the name

Fairfax, which comes from the motto of the family: "*Fare, fac*," or say, do. The other syllable, *fair* or *far*, found in so many names, like *Fairman*, *Playfair*, *Fairchild*, *Farwell*, *Farnum*, etc., is especially troublesome. It may be from the Saxon *fair*, meaning beautiful, clear, just; or it may be from the Saxon *faren*, to travel; or the German *fern*, distant; or the English *far* or *fern;* or the Norman *Frère*, brother; or the Latin *facere*, to do, or *fari*, to speak. The ancient spelling or some extraneous information will frequently afford a clew in investigations of this sort, but numerous insolvable cases remain. If it were not for questions of this nature etymology would be a comparatively simple matter, and would possess an element of certainty which would deprive it of much of its charm.

Surnames came into general use very slowly. We may say, broadly, that the introduction of the surname—as we understand the term, a name common to all the children of a family—dates from the tenth century, and was not general before the fourteenth century. Indeed, there were districts in Wales in the last generation where individuals possessed but one name. Now it has become difficult for a man to change his surname. Tyrwhitt says in his edition of Chaucer: "It is probable that the use of surnames was not in Chaucer's time fully established among the lower class of people," and Lower, in his work on surnames, holds that hereditary surnames can scarcely be said to have been permanently settled among the lower class before the era of the Reformation. Among the upper classes the name of the estate descended from father to son and served as a distinctive appellation, but the pedigree of the Fitz-Hugh family runs thus through nine generations:

    Bardolph.
    Akaris Fitz-Bardolph.
    Hervey Fitz-Akaris.
    Henry Fitz-Hervey.
    Randolph Fitz-Henry.
    Henry Fitz-Randolph.
    Randolph Fitz-Henry.
    Hugh Fitz-Randolph.
    Henry Fitz-Hugh.

This last Henry assumed the name, Fitz-Hugh, and gave it permanence as a family application in the reign of Edward III. In the same reign (1340) we find the following in a list of the commonalty:

    Johannes over the Water.
    William at Bishope Gate.
    Johannes o' the Shephouse.
    Agnes the Priest's Sister.
    Johannes in the Lane.

Johannes at See.
Johannes le Taillour.
Johannes of the Gutter.

This shows that surnames were not universal in the fourteenth century. The growth of civilization making it necessary to identify every person, and confusion arising from the multiplication of the baptismal names, men were forced to use some sobriquet as a distinctive mark. By degrees these became firmly attached surnames. For a long period it was legal for a man to change his surname, but not his baptismal name. Lord Coke holds this distinctly. While the oldest son among the Normans in England assumed the name of the paternal estate, the younger sons not infrequently assumed entirely different ones on acquiring land in other counties. Thus Richard, Earl of Brionne, has five names in Domesday Book (the list of knights who accompanied the Conqueror). He is called:

1. Richard de Tourbridge, from a lordship in Kent.
2. Richard de Benfeld.
3. Richard de Benefacta.
4. Richard de Clare, from a Suffolk lordship.
5. Richard Fitz-Gilbert, from his father's name.

To go back a step further, we find that as a rule our Saxon ancestors were content with but one name, as Gurth, or Cedric, or Alfred. To avoid confusion, they sometimes distinguished two men of the same name by adding the tribal name, usually ending in *ing* or the father's given name. Sometimes a descriptive appellation was used, as: Harold Harefoot, Edmund Ironsides, Edward the Confessor, Edith Swansneck; and Bede tells us of two priests named Hewald, "whom," he says, "we distinguished as Hewald Black and Hewald White, by reason of the difference in color of their hair." From this early time when two names * were unusual, comes the habit, still surviving, of calling sovereigns by their single baptismal name. English bishops still sign their Christian names and the names of their sees to all documents. That the first names of the contracting parties are used in the marriage service is also an ancient survival.

A classification of surnames by their derivations gives us four principal classes: †

First; surnames derived from personal names.

---

*When a missionary baptized, as we are told was the case, an entire company of men John, and an equal number of women Catharine, some distinctive nicknames, or eke names, would be absolutely necessary.

† Thirty years ago the negroes in the south had no real surnames, and even now they change their names with great readiness.

These nearly always take the patronymic form, as Henrickson or MacAdam. But in a few cases the given name of the father has been adopted as a family name; thus we have Henry George, Patrick Henry, Henry James, William Paul, and a few others.

Second; local surnames. These are derived from an estate, manor, or village, or from some natural feature of the earth, as Henry Hill, David Dudley Field, William Wood, Henry Yorke, John Worthington.

Third; occupative surnames, drawn from some trade or office. This is a very numerous class. We find Carpenters, Taylors, Smiths, Websters, Turners, and Wrights, or Stewarts, Butlers, and Chamberlains everywhere.

Fourth; surnames derived from personal peculiarities, from nicknames, from some fancied resemblance to a bird or to an animal. Thus we have White, Brown, Black or Blake, Talman, Armstrong, Crookshanks, Lamb, Cow, Fox, etc. Into this class must come those names derived from business signs, from heraldic animals pictured on coats of arms, and from family mottoes. Of such a name as Lion, or Bull, we cannot say whether it was first given by reason of the strength or courage of the man originally bearing it, or because he was the landlord of an inn having the beast on its sign. Names of this derivation might properly come under class three; but as this derivation is rarely certain, we are obliged to put them in class four.

From names formed in any of these four ways patronymics might be formed. The son of William the Clerk might be called John Clarkson; of George Brown, Henry Brownson or Brunson. John gives us Johnson, Johns, and Jones. Daw, the short for David, gives us Dawson, and Lamb, Lampson. The territorial appellative, Whitby, is the source of the family name Whitbyson. Patronymics formed from territorial names are rare, but they are very generally formed from personal names. Thus twenty-four forms come from William: Williams, Williamson, Wills, Wilks, Wilkins, Wilkinson, Wickens, Wickenson, Bill, Bilson, Wilson, Woolson, Woolcock, Woolcot, Wooley, Wilcoxe, Wilcoxson, Wilcoxon, Willet, Willy, Willis, Wilsie, Wylie, Willott, and probably Woolsey. Most of these are patronymics, though some are diminutives. Woolcot and Willcox, for instance, mean little Will, and might have been applied to a diminutive person, as well as to a child.

The Gaelic patronymic prefix is *Mac* or *O;* the Cymric is *O* or *Ap*. In Ireland *O* meant grandson, or, in a more enlarged sense, any male descendant. *Mac* meant son. The *O* is supposed in Ireland to be more ancient than the *Mac*, and is more common. With the exception of O'Gowan,* it is not found attached to any industrial name, which may account for the idea that it is considered the more honorable prefix. Both these prefixes designate not only the children of a family, but the members of a clan. *Clan* means children. In Gaelic Scotland the *Mac* only was used. But the members of a clan were only theoretically blood-relations, not necessarily so. The Norman *Fitz* and the Danish *Son* mean son of the blood. The Welsh also used the genitive *s*, as in Williams, Davids, Jones, to designate the son, though *ap* was their ancient form. The Saxon suffix *ing* was a tribal patronymic. We see it in *Waring, Alling*, or *Billings*, where it has the meaning of the "descendants of." It is the oldest and rarest patronymic in use, though the Celtic *O* may lay claim to equal antiquity. The Cymric patronymic *Ap* is usually amalgamated with the personal name. Thus Price is *Ap Rice*, the son of *Rhys;* Pugh is *Ap Hugh*, Powell is *Ap Howell*, Bowen is *Ap Owen*, Pritchard is *Ap Richard*, Bethell is *Ap Ithell*, Bevan is *Ap Evan*, and as *Evan* and *Ivan* are forms of John, Bevan is the same name as Johnson or Jones, which is really Johns. Most of the names beginning in *Ap* are Welsh, like Apple-

* Gowan means a smith.

gate, *Ap Legatt;* Appleyard, *Ap Ledyard,* and *Apthorp.** The distinctively Welsh names are Owens, Davis, Morgan, Howell, Jones, and Williams.

To return to our first class of surnames, those derived directly from personal names, one of the first things that strikes us as peculiar about the English is their inveterate habit of shortening the given name of a man to, if possible, one syllable. Thus, if a man were christened Bartholomew they called him Bat, from whence come the surnames Bates, Bartlette, and Babcock. The suffixes *cock, got, lot,* and *kin* were diminutives of good-fellowship or of endearment. The syllables appear in many of our surnames, as Wilkins, Wilcox, Simcox. *Cock* is seen also in the expressions *cock*-robin, *cock*-sparrow. *Cock*-robin in the nursery song does not necessarily mean male robin, but quite as much, dear little robin. Matilda, shortened to Till, was made Tillot, and Tillot and Tillotson are used as surnames, for there are a few matronymics to be found in English. Margaret was shortened to Margot, and we find the rare name Margotson. Walter was Wat, whence Watts and Watson. John was Jack, whence Jackson. Robert was shortened

* Apthorpe, however, is thought to be Atthorpe, or of the village ; Appleton and Applegarth are compounded of Apple and the Saxon syllables, *ton* or *garth.*

to Robin, Rob, Dob, and Dod, whence Robertson, Robinson, Robeson, Dobson, and Dodson. David was Daw, whence Dawson, and Horace was Hod, whence Hodson. From Isaac comes Hick, hence Hicks and Hixson and Hitchcock; from Gilbert, Gib and Gibson. No other nation exercises this unlicensed habit of deforming given names. The Frenchman certainly pronounces his name—Emile, Leon, or Adolphe—in full. Nicknames are given, it is true, by all nations. A nickname is an *eke name*, or an additional name invented in a jesting spirit, and must not be confounded with a shortened given name.

A patronymic is pretty sure to date back to the sixteenth century, if not to a much earlier period. The old Bible Christian names, like Samuel, Jacob, Daniel, Peter, John, and James, have all given us patronymic derivatives. Joseph, too, appears in Jessop. But the Bible names adopted in the seventeenth century by the Puritans, like Asa, Abijah, Seth, Eli, Jabez, have not resulted in any patronymics, because they were taken up after surnames were pretty well settled. Some personal names that have disappeared from use are preserved in patronymics. The Norman names Ivo, Hugo, Hammet, once so common, are now never given to English-speaking boys, but survive in the surnames Ives, Iveson,

Hughes and *Hamlin*.* The very pretty girl-names, Joyce, *joyeuse*, or merry; Lettice, *Letitia*, or innocent pleasure; and, best of all, *Hilary*, from the root of hilarious or happy, now lost, might very properly be revived in use.

The second division is local or territorial surnames. Barons to whom a grant of land was made usually took the name of the town or estate which was their foef. In French-English names this is generally evidenced by the prefix *de*, which we see in the names *Devereux, Delafield, Delameter, Delaney, Delancey*, etc. Then, again, nothing was more natural than to call a man after the place of his abode, as John of the Mill, William at the Brook or River. *Atwood, Atwater, Woods* and *Waters, Nash* or *Aten-Ash, Nokes* or *Atten-Oaks, Green, Lane, Townsend, Shaw, Lay*, or *Leigh*, and *Dean* are local names. A *shaw* was a small thick wood; a *dean* or *den* was a wooded valley, and a *lay* or *lea* was a pasture. *Dean*, like *Parsons*, might also be derived from an ecclesiastical title. *Graves* is the same as *Groves*. *Cliffe, Clifford*, and *Cleveland* are of substantially the same meaning. Any name ending in *thwait*, an enclosure; *ton* or *by*, a town; *combe*, a ridge; *throp* or *thorpe* or *ville*, a village;

---

* Hugo, however, appears in Hugh, and Hamelin, a little town or hamlet, may be a duplicate source for Hamlin.

ham, a home; *ly* or *ey*, an island; or *ford*, a path, is pretty certain to be a territorial name. From the cathedrals we have the names *St. Omers*, or Sommers; *St. Denis*, or Sidney; *St. Clair*, or Sinclair, etc., though names of this denomination may have been (in some instances) derived from the motto or family war-cry embodying the name of the patron saint. From the points of the compass we have *North*, *Norris*, *South*, *Southey*, *Surrey*, *West*, *Wesley*, *East*, *Easterly*, and *Sterling*. *Wallace* and *L'Estrange*, meaning a foreigner, evidently have reference to the place of abode, though, strictly speaking, not local names.

From the names of countries we have *Irish*, *Scott*, *French*, *Brett* and *Britton* from Brittany, *Burgoyne* from Burgundy, *Gale* from Gael, *Janeway* from Genoese, *Norman* from Normandy, *Saxon*, *Wales*, and *Morris*.*

Bottom is the old Sussex word for valley, and is compounded in a number of English names, as Higgin*bothem*, Winter*bottom*, etc. *Burne* is a brook; *Clough*, a ravine; *Cobb*, a harbor; *Crouch*, a cross, of which so many were erected in the market-places of towns. *Hatch* is a gate; *Holt* is a grove; *Lynch*, a thicket; *Ross*, a heath; *Sykes*, a spring; *Sale*, a hall. These are all territorial

---

* Morris and Moore have several derivations: Moor, a plain; Moor, an Arab; Mohr, great, etc.

names, though *Ross* may be, in some instances, from the word meaning red.

The names of places and persons not unfrequently end in *ham, ingham,* or *ington.* These are true Saxon territorial names. The termination *ing* meant belonging to the tribe. Thus, *King* is really son of the tribe. The Eppings and Hastings are the descendants of *Aes,* the Warings of *Waer,* the Erpings of *Erp,* and so on through some two hundred and fifty monosyllabic given names. Very few of these words ending in *ing* are found to-day in England as surnames, because the custom of adopting transmissible family appellations was not instituted in Saxon England; but all of them have given names to English villages, though usually the suffix *ton,* town, or *ham,* home, is added. Thus *Walsingham* is the home of the Walsing; *Worthington* is the town of the Worthing. Then, these towns gave surnames to those who lived in them, and we have the class of old Saxon names like Remington, Hoisington, Huntington, Allington, Erpingham, Buckingham, Washington, and many others. These are the finest names in our language. *Coffin,* which is seen in Covington, is the only one not strong and euphonic. In addition to these, there is hardly to be found a town or county that has not given a surname to some families. York, Bradford, Manchester, Winchester, Sheffield, Kent, Salisbury, Richmond, Chester, we meet everywhere.

Of the third class, or occupative surnames, we have a large number, and as a rule these surnames are represented by a larger number of individuals than are any others. The *Smith* was, of course, represented in every village, though he is sometimes called a *Gower* or a *Gowan* in Celtic districts. Then we have *Bishops, Clerks, Parsons, Leaches, Carters, Tailors, Turners, Cooks, Fullers* or cloth-workers, *Carpenters, Wagners, Millers, Wrights,* etc., in abundance. We have no doctors nor lawyers, though *Councilman* is not unknown, nor is *Judge* as a surname. *Spenser* is *dispensier*, the man who had charge of the spence or buttery. *Stewart* is the king's steward, and *Butler* his "boteler." Many old forgotten trades are represented in occupative surnames. *Scudder* is probably *Scuteler*, the man who made the wooden trenchers — *scutels* — which served instead of plates. *Latimer*, or *Latiner*, is an interpreter; *Pullinger* — *boulanger* — is a baker; *Jenner* is a joiner. In Yorkshire, *Sack* means a ploughshare, and from this comes Sacksmith, or Sixsmith. *Kidder* is an obsolete word for huckster. No one can make anything of *Lundhunter*. *Brewer, Brewster, Weaver, Webb, Webster, Baker,* and *Baxter* are plain enough. *Walker* was a man who inspected the king's forest and guarded the game from poachers. *Dexter* appears to be from *daegsestre*, a woman who works by the day, or, possibly, from the word meaning a maker of daggers.

A *Pilgrim* was one who had taken a journey to any shrine, as to Canterbury. A *Palmer* was one who had gone to Palestine. There were so many pilgrims that it was not used as a distinctive name, but to be a "holy palmer" was an honor. The *porter* "stood at the castle gate," the *usher* within. Now there are many Porters, but few Ushers. The reason of this is that Porter had an additional source—from the porters who carried burdens. The *Hayward*—from *hay*, a hedge—had charge of the animals belonging to the town. *Howard* is derived from this word, unless it be from the Saxon *Hereward*, or general. *Hogward* gives us *Haggard*, a very rare surname. *Wirth* and *Ward* are the terms for Saxon officials often found in combination in surnames, as Woods*worth*, Wood*ward*, etc. A *Barker* is a tanner.

The fourth class comprises surnames derived from nicknames. To call individuals by some personal peculiarity is a very natural propensity. The Romans and the modern Italians seem especially fond of doing so. The English working-men in some districts still have two names— one their regular legal name, which is seldom heard, and another, the nickname by which they are known among their mates. It was inevitable that surnames should grow out of those sobriquets, which are often more firmly attached than the baptismal name itself. Nicknames can be conveniently divided into three groups:

1. Those from physical or external peculiarities, relationship, age, size, shape, complexion, dress, etc.

2. From mental and moral peculiarities. Sometimes these are complimentary, sometimes quite the reverse.

3. Real nicknames, having no especial meaning, or from some fancied resemblance to animals.

Under the first sub-head we have *White, Brown, Black, Grey, Morrell* or *Moore*—when it means black; *Nott*, which means crop-haired; *Peel*, which means pilled or bald; *Russell* or red, and a variety of others. *Frieze-mantle* is the origin of the name Freemantle. *Bunker* means *Bon Couleur*. *Big* and *Small* and *Little* and *Pettit* explain themselves. The odd name *Firebraces* is derived from *Bras de fer* (iron arm) by inversion. We have, too, *Younger, Senior, Ames*, from *Eam* (an uncle), *Kinsman*, and *Cozzens*.

Under the second sub-head we have *Good, Fairspeech, Pinchpenny, Saveall, Scrapeskin*, etc.

The third sub-head, or nicknames proper, presents considerable difficulties. The nickname may have been meaningless, or it may have become obsolete, and if the spelling has been changed we have nothing to aid us in reconstructing it. When we find a name that seems absolutely unexplainable, it is convenient to be able to say that the base is probably an unmeaning sobriquet. The names which sound like the names of animals — as *Bull, Lamb, Wolf, Lion, Crow, Swan, Hart, Stagg*—may possibly have originated in nicknames, and afterwards have developed into surnames, but it is much more likely that they originated in heraldic devices or business signs. Every little manufactory had its device—a ship, or an arrow, or a rudely-carved lion or bull's head. The proprietor was spoken of as William of the Ship, or John o' the Lion.. Inn signs were generally double—a device on each side, or a line divided the field, as in the shields of knights. Thus we have the "Goat and Compasses," the "Cat and Battledoor," the "Bull and Mouth," "Pan and the Bacchanalians"—this last corrupted into "Pan and the Bag o' Nails." As a rule, heraldic devices were borne by families who took the name of an estate, and the names of animals given as nicknames for fancied resemblance in strength or swiftness are inextricably mixed up with the same names drawn from business signs in the twelfth and thirteenth centuries.

The number of names in each of the above classes varies greatly. Taking a large number of names in the *London Directory*, it was computed that about twenty-five per cent. were from personal names, thirty-three per cent. were local, twelve per cent. occupative, twenty-five per cent. from nicknames, leaving five per cent. unaccounted for and unaccountable. The number of individuals in each class would differ greatly from these ratios, if for no other reason, because a disproportionate number of persons bear the names of occupation. *Smith, Taylor, Carpenter, Webster, Baker,* and the like, and the personal derivatives, *Johnson, Thompson, Jones, Williams,* are also very well represented. No one territorial surname is borne by a great number of persons. *White* and *Brown* are also very common.

The question arises—Is the number of surnames increasing or diminishing? We hear occasionally of families becoming extinct by the death of the "last of the name." On the other hand, a few new surnames are formed even now by variations in spelling or the anglicizing of foreign names. The entire disappearance of a name is rarer than we think, as it will generally be found that it is preserved in the family of some remote and forgotten offshoot. The practice of hyphenating names like "Floyd-Jones" may give rise to some new variants. The doctrine of chances proves that it is extremely improbable that any name that has lasted from the fourteenth century to the present should become extinct hereafter. Furthermore, observations on sixty names in England go to show that the excess of births over deaths in any group bearing the same name is normal, or the same as that of the great bulk of the population.

It has been computed from a careful tabulation of the surnames beginning with "A" that the entire number of surnames in England would exceed thirty thousand. In our country the large foreign element would make the number still greater, even admitting that many rare English names are unrepresented here, and that many foreign names have been assimilated in sound and spelling to our American surnames.

The thirty names most common in England are given in the following table from *Patronymica Britannica*, in the order of their frequency:

1. Smith, one in every 73 of entire population.
2. Jones, " " 76 " "
3. Williams, " " 115 " "
4. Taylor, " " 148 " "
5. Davies, " " 162 " "
6. Brown, " " 174 " "
7. Thomas, " " 196 " "

8. Evans, one in every 198 of entire population.
9. Roberts, " " 235 " "
10. Johnson, " " 265 " "
11. Wilson, " " 275 " "
12. Robinson, " " 276 " "
13. Wright, " " 293 " "
14. Wood, " " 301 " "
15. Thompson," " 304 " "
16. Hall, " " 305 " "
17. Walker, " " 310 " "
18. Green, " " 310 " "
19. Hughes, " " 312 " "
20. Edwards, " " 316 " "
21. Lewis, " " 318 " "
22. White, " " 323 " "
23. Turner, " " 327 " "
24. Jackson, " " 330 " "
25. Hill, " " 352 " "
26. Harris, " " 355 " . "
27. Clark, " " 363 " "
28. Cooper, " " 380 " "
29. Harrison, " " 390 " "
30. Ward, " " 402 " "

These thirty names are applied to a little more than one-sixth of the entire population of England. The Welsh name *Davies* is distinct from *Davis*, which has one representative in every four hundred and twenty-one Englishmen. This name, and *Jones, Williams, Evans, Owens,* and *Edwards* are common names, because there are so few Welsh surnames. It is said that *Evan Evans*— or its equivalent, *John Jones*—is so common in Wales that it does not individualize its owner in the least.

Those who wish to look up this subject more fully are referred to Lower's Dictionary, the *Patronymica Britannica*, to the *Essay on English Surnames*, and to *The Teutonic Name System*, by the same author. These contain a great deal of curious information. In the introduction to the first-named is an account of the older authorities, many of whom are very entertaining. Robert Ferguson's book, *Surnames as a Science*, is more modern (1883), and, though treating of but a limited number of names, more systematic. An earlier work by the same author, *English Surnames*, may also be consulted. Bardsley's *English Surnames* is entertaining, but limited. Bowditch's *Suffolk Surnames* (third edition) contains a long list of peculiar names found in this country, but the author seems more occupied with the humors and oddities of the directories than with scientific examination or classification. For given names Miss Yonge's two volumes on *Christian Names* cover a good deal of ground. The Appendix to *Webster's Dictionary* will also be found useful.

CHAPTER XVI.

WORDS OF THE PROFESSIONS AND TRADES.

To the philologist the meanings of words are of comparatively little importance except as a means of identification. He follows the root through its various fortunes, pointing out how it has gathered suffixes and prefixes and amalgamated with them, or dropped them in the course of centuries until the original sound is entirely changed and the word becomes part of a new language—becomes, in fact, a new word. But a great deal of interesting information about the early professions and trades can be gathered by observing the peculiar vocabulary of each. Such an examination carried but a little way will throw incidentally a good deal of light on history, and will show how men instinctively select a set of words having a relation to the nature of their employments. In all the mechanical trades technical terms are used which are interesting survivals of ancient usage, and others which show when improvements in tools or methods were introduced. Let us consider first the ancient and honorable trade of the smith.

The worker in iron was an important member of society in the early village communities. He forged the rude weapons and agricultural implements, shod the horses, and made the hasps, hinges, and nails requisite to building a house. In making armor great proficiency was required, and in forging railings, screens, and ornamental work a high degree of artistic skill was often shown. There is nothing more satisfying to the artistic sense than finely-wrought iron-work, as there is nothing more unsatisfying than cast-iron ornaments. One is the product of human intelligence, subduing an obdurate material directly by strength, patience, and skill; the other is mechanically produced after the pattern is made, and has therefore a much less direct relation to the human mind. For all these reasons the workman in iron held in early days a unique position. He was not called a *smith* because he was a *smiter*, as was originally supposed. *Smith* is one of the oldest Teutonic words, and is probably connected with *smooth*. But his helper is called a *striker*. To *smith* a piece of iron is to form it with the hammer; but to *forge* includes the idea of heating in addition. The worker in brass is not a smith, but a *brass-founder*, because brass is melted, and if wrought is hammered with light blows. We have *copper-smith, gold-smith, silver-smith,* and *tin-smith,* because these metals are ductile and require smithing. The word had many metaphorical applications in early literature. Not only do we read of the armorer by the name of *waepna-smith,* but we have the promoter of laughter called *hleahtor-smith,* laughter-smith; we have the teacher called *lár-smith,* lore-smith; and the warrior called *wíg-smith,* war-smith.* The scales which fell from the iron were called *slag,* because they were slugged from under the sledge. Nowadays we apply the term *slag* to the impurities which float on molten iron, as blast-furnace slag. Etymologically it would be more correct to call this substance by the original name, *sinner* or *cinder,* a term which we are inclined to confine to the calcined impurities in coal-ashes. The old terms are correctly used by the hands in a rolling-mill, where they speak of *hammer-slag,* and call refuse that is melted and squeezed out, cinder, not cinders, even saying "*roller cinder.*"

The following are some of the terms used by

---

* The fact that now the word *sharp* would be used in folk-metaphor for many of the above meanings—the teacher, for instance, called the book-*sharp;* the musician, the piano-*sharp;* the geologist, the rock-*sharp*—may be taken as illustrative of the difference between ancient and modern times, the days of honest blows and the days of shifty devices.

the smith : *bellows, wind, tuyere, anvil, blast, hammer, tap, screw, tongs, fire, sledge, swedge, file, horn, upset, weld, flatter.* He uses the word *wind* in the sense of air, and speaks of the *wind* in the bellows as he might speak of "knocking the wind" out of an antagonist, not the atmosphere. The moving or issuing air he calls the *blast*. These words are of Scandinavian or Anglo-Saxon origin, and show that the Germanic tribes were skilful workers in iron before they came into contact with the Latin races, and, further, that blacksmiths continued to use their trade-terms after the Conquest, without much reference to the language* of the Norman-French. The words *former, vice,* and *die* are Norman, but they are special tools, adapted to produce certain shapes more readily than can the hammer. *Chisel* is Norman, but even now a blacksmith calls the stationary chisel fitted into a square hole in the anvil, preferably, a *cutter.* The hole in the anvil has also a peculiar name, used by some blacksmiths. It

---

* The back of the hammer is called by mechanics the *pene,* and to straighten a piece of iron by light blows with the sharp back on the hollow side is said to be to *pene* it. This word is given in *Webster* as *pin,* as if connected with the Latin *pinna,* which seems impossible, whether we regard pronunciation, meaning, or probable source. *Monkeywrench* is another very peculiar expression. None of the explanations offered concerning its origin seem entirely satisfactory.

would be worth while to collect all the blacksmith's words—many of which are not in the dictionary —and also to ascertain whether some words are not in use in this country that have been lost in England. In general the smiths of England use more archaic words than do those of America, as so many new devices to save hand labor are in use here.

The distinctive names of the parts of the steam-engine were, for the most part, taken from those of similar parts of a pump—an instrument which was known to the Romans—so that we find *steam-chest, piston, cylinder, valve, governor, connecting-rod, crank, main-shaft, balance-wheel, exhaust-pipe, eccentric, cross-head, stuffing-box, gland, parallel-motion, slides*, representing a very large proportion of words of Latin derivation, as might be expected, since the steam-engine was invented by men acquainted with the use of scientific instruments, and at a time when Latin terms had been fully naturalized. Even English George Stephenson's machine was called a *locomotive*, though the starting-valve is still properly the *throttle*. Many of the smaller parts of the construction—*key, cotters, gibs*, well-known mechanical devices of great antiquity, and adapted to the new purpose by mechanics—have Saxon names, but as far as the engine is a "thermodynamic machine," its nomenclature is Latin. The compound name, *steam-engine*, is half English and half Latin.

As the art of printing was invented in Germany and brought to England through Holland, we might expect to find in its vocabulary a large proportion of Teutonic words. So far is this from being the case that there is no trade of which the nomenclature is so distinctively Latin. The man who arranges the *types* is called a *compositor*. He takes the types from a *case*, and places them in a *stick*, brings his stickfuls to a *galley*, puts them on an *imposing-stone*, and takes an *impression*, which he calls a *proof;* *corrects* the proof, and locks the type in a *form* with *quoins*. Then, the proof-reader's marks are all Latin abbreviations, and the different sizes of type, *pica*, *primer*, *minion*, *brevier*, and *agate*, are all called by Latin names, and the same is true of the elementary parts of the press except the *bed*. In fact, so thoroughly Latin is the printer's vocabulary that he must be conscious of falling below the dignity of his trade when he asks for a *take* or speaks of *pulling* a proof, or calls blank spaces *fat*. He *justifies* his lines by *spaces*, the last being almost the only Saxon word he habitually uses. *Quad* is *quadrate*, a square space. The *pages* are collected into *signatures*, and the types are finally *distributed* after the *printing*. *Ink*, too, is a Romance word—*en caustre*—though adopted into old English. In fact, the technical vocabulary of the printer is as Latin as that of the lawyer. The reason of this is that the first printers were learned men, and Latin was the language of scholars in the fifteenth century. They were the successors of the old scribes. Caxton personally translated from Latin a number of the books he published—and the best work of the early printers was editions of the classics. Printing was not supposed to be a people's art, nor could any one have foreseen that it was to be one of the great popular forces. So its language is scholastic, and in the dialect of those for whose service it was intended.

The trade of making and repairing coverings for the feet is an old one in cold countries; so we find that those following it are *cobblers* and *shoemakers*, not *chaussiers*, and may be pretty sure that our Saxon ancestors did not go barefooted at all times. *Cobbler* is given by Skeat as from *couplare*, to join,* as if a cobbler were one who joins new leather to old, and was a Norman. This derivation does not seem consistent with the character of the word nor with the fact that it contains two *b*'s, nor with the fact that the cobbler's tools have all Celtic or Saxon names. There is a flavor

---

* See discussion of this word in *Century Dictionary*, and in Dr. Murray's *Dictionary*.

about the word which does not belong to a Latin derivative. It sounds like an old folk-word. It is the same word as that found in *cobble-stones*, with which we cobble or roughly mend a wall.* *Shoemaker*, at all events, is above suspicion as to its genuinely English source, and so are the shoemaker's terms. His *kit* is a small receptacle for tools; we have the same word in "kit of mackerel." His *last* is from a Saxon word meaning a track, connected in root with the word to *last*—to endure; to *pursue* is the same as to track, and to pursue unceasingly implies endurance; so there is a distant connection between the two meanings of *last*. *Vamp* is said to be derived from *avant-pied*, the front foot, but the uppers were first made from a single piece, Latimer says. So *vamp* is a modern word. *Welt* may be of Celtic origin, and *lace* may be descended from the Latin *laqueus*, a snare, though this seems hardly probable in the sense of boot-lace. *Awl, lapstone, waxed ends, leather, hide, pegs, patch, sole*, are all of Teutonic origin. *Tan*, if not from an English root, has been used so long that it may be regarded as an original English word. *Kip-skin* and *deacon's-skin* are undoubtedly English, though their derivations

* Why should it not be distantly connected with *cobble*, a boat (Celtic)? The wooden shoes of the French peasantry are hollowed out like boats, and *cobble*, a boat, is based on the word meaning to excavate.

are not known. *Tap*, so universally used for half-sole, and seen in the old phrase, "standing on his *taps*," must mean either the *top* sole, or else a sole that is fastened on with pegs which are driven in by taps of the hammer. *Foxing*, or putting a front on a boot, is an old English word. *Boots* and *gaiters* are of course comparatively modern, for our ancestors wore shoes. Many of these words were not printed nor written, unless they may have appeared in some of the Elizabethan dramas, and as we do not know the original spelling, the derivations may be lost. It is evident, however, that the shoemaker has plied his trade and used the same words for his implements and materials since our ancestors emigrated from Schleswig-Holstein.

The building trades—masons and wood-workers —would evidently be much more affected by the conquest of England by a people speaking a foreign language than would the folk-trades—village smiths and cobblers and household-weavers. The Normans were skilful architects, especially in stone, and built feudal castles, extensive ecclesiastical buildings—cathedrals and monasteries. Most of the important buildings were erected under a Norman master, or in the cities where French was spoken by the wealthy classes. The old word *wright* was dropped, except in some special cases, like *wainwright, wheelwright, mill-*

wright, playwright, and a few others. When Chaucer says of one of his pilgrims:

"He was a well good *wrighte*, a carpentere,"

he may be using *wright* as we should use mechanic—as a general term—or he may feel it necessary to explain a Saxon word by the equivalent Norman word. However this may be, we find all through the vocabulary of these trades a mixture of English and French words, the French being usually applied to special tools and to work of a higher grade, and the English to simpler and more elementary operations. *Carpenter, joiner*, and *mason* are French words. *Builder* and *stone-cutter* are English. *House* and *home* and *cottage* are English, and so are the elementary parts of a simple building: the *doors, roof, nails, walls*,* *sills, eaves, beams, rafters, thatch, shingles, boards, laths, scantling, timber, floor*. On the other hand, the *joist*, from *jacere*, to lie; the *studding*, from *sto*, to stand; the *posts*, from *posita*, the *planks*, the *plates*, the *jambs*, are all Norman, and the Norman mansion is divided into rooms and chambers. The *chimney* is Norman, and so is the *flue*. The Saxons apparently built a *fireplace*, a *hearth*, and a *hob*,

---

* *Wall* is from *vallum*, but is Latin of the first period, not Norman. *Sleeper* is another Teutonic word, connected with *slab*. *Sleeper* from *slape*—a smooth foundation—not from lying still, as if sleeping.

and let the smoke escape from a hole in the roof, or a *window* (*wind-eye*). All the ornamental and architectural parts of a house are Norman, and so is any complicated construction, and so, of course, are all the parts of a cathedral. Possibly some of these architectural terms were introduced into England by foreign workmen before the Conquest, like *tower*, and a few of the oldest words connected with church architecture. On the whole, the relations of the races are very strikingly illustrated in the names of the parts of a building.

There are three words in common use by carpenters and woodsmen in America, which are no doubt survivals of old words: *brash, stunt,* and *dozy*. *Brash* is an adjective applied to wood which is lacking in transverse strength and elasticity. A "*brash* stick" differs from a brittle one in that it will not spring or bend at all. This word is referred to in *Webster* as being of Armorican origin. The application of *brash*—also very common—to quick temper—giving away suddenly and unexpectedly—is possibly secondary. *Stunt* means cut at an obtuse angle with the grain, bluntly sharpened. It is connected with *stint*, to make short, but retains the original meaning of "making dull"—as in "that post is too *stunt* to drive"—rather than of cutting off a definite portion, as in the expression, "a day's *stint*." *Dozy* means affected by a peculiar kind of rot which destroys the grain. If so far gone as to be ruined by the dry-rot, timber is said to be *punky*, which is from the Gaelic *spunk*, tinder. *Dozy* means in the incipient state of dry-rot when the "life of the timber is gone." It is probably connected with *dozy*, sleepy. *Skeat* says of *dozy*, meaning sleepy, " cf. Sanscrit *dhoas*, to crumble." Crumbling would almost exactly hit the carpenter's use of *dozy*.

In the names of wood-workers' tools we find that the simpler and more general tools have English names, and that those adapted for some special purpose are Norman. The *axe* is the most important and primitive tool that man uses. A skilful axeman can shape almost anything from wood, as is seen to-day in Russia. The *axe* is so archaic an implement that its name is similar in all the Aryan languages, showing that its use was understood even before the Germanic and Italic stocks developed definitely different languages. We retain the name of the tool that was used to hew the timber for the ships that brought Hengist and Horsa to Britain, and have borrowed from the French only the diminutive form, *hatchet*, and the verb to *hatch*—*i.e.*, to mark with cross-lines — corresponding to our English verb, to *score*, and *hash*, anything chopped up. The *saw* is, of course, not nearly so old a tool as the axe, which indeed dates from the Stone Age, but our Saxon ancestors possessed it and called it a *sage*, and we use the same word. The primitive operations, *chopping*, *hewing*, *cutting*, *splitting*, and *riving* are all indicated by Saxon words. It is worth noticing that in many parts of the country the modern workman uses the word *split* when he separates a piece of irregular shape, and the word *rive* when he separates a wide thin piece, the taking special pains seeming to be the distinction. Thus he *splits* wood, but he *rives* a bolt to make shingles. The word *bolt* in the above sense is no doubt equivalent to *billet*. *Drawshave*, *grindstone*, *whetstone*, *hammer*, *saw*, *adze*, and *axe*, are all English, but *plane*, *chisel*, *gouge*, *mortice*, and *tenon*, are all French. A carpenter to-day calls a small plane used for cutting a groove by the French name, *rabot*, or *rabbeting-plane*, from the French *raboter*, to plane. *Mitre* is French, and means properly to cut at an angle of forty-five degrees, a word derived from the bishop's hat; but the Saxon word *scarf* means to hew at any sharp angle with an axe. *Auger* and *gimlet* are English, as might be expected, since the simplest construction necessitates boring holes. We know that the English built ships, of which the framing and planking were secured with pins called *treenails*, and with leathern thongs. The long plane which is used for making the edges of boards straight is called a *jointer*, from *joindre*, to unite, since the edges when brought together come in contact throughout and can be firmly united with glue. The word *joint* refers to an inflexible union, though we use it preferably for a flexible one, as the joints of the body.

The mixed vocabulary of the carpenter's trade goes to show that the Saxons were competent wood-workers before the Conquest, but that the Norman workmen modified their method by introducing better tools and a higher order of architecture. The same may be said of stone-masons and plasterers, who have preserved some singular words like *hawk*,* the board on which they carry mortar; *darby*, a board for smoothing the face of a wall; and *putlog* and *ledger* for parts of the scaffold.

Cast-iron was not invented till the seventeenth century, but the art of casting brass was known to the ancients. The technical name of the pot in which brass is melted is *crucible*. The establishment for making iron castings is a *foundery*. Both of those are French words, *crucible* being probably of Celtic origin and connected with

---

* The derivation of *hawk* and *darby* I am unable to conjecture. *Hawk*, to carry about, seems to imply the idea of offering for sale. Can *darby* be connected with *daub?* The carpenters pronounce jointer *jinter*. As this is the archaic pronunciation correctly handed down, have we any right to change it?

crock. But many of the words used by men who work in a foundery are English. They are called *moulders*. The sand is rammed in a *flask*, of which the top is called the *cope* or *nowl* (one word being French, the other Saxon) and the bottom the *drag*. The opening through which the metal enters the mould is called a *gate*, and the metal which hardens in the gate is called a *sprue*. The division in the mould is called a *parting*, the vessel in which the melted metal is received from the furnace is called a *ladle*. The large sieve used to separate lumps from the sand is called a *riddle*, a small tool for smoothing the mould is a *slick*, and the waste metal which runs into the parting is a *fin*. The patterns are made with *draft* that they may be readily drawn from the sand, and a *shrink-rule* is used by pattern-makers. Here is a large proportion of Saxon words, all of them, however, except *sprue*, used in secondary senses—*riddle*, for instance, is originally a winnowing sieve. The art was developed among an English-speaking people by practical men, not by scientific men. These men naturally took up popular words, whereas the inventors of the steam-engine used learned words. Had iron-founding developed from the casting of brass, more of the technical words would have been of Latin origin. Had it been an old English art, it would have contained more old English words belonging exclusively to its peculiar operations. *Sprue* seems to be the only special term.

The Saxons were seamen, but so were the early Normans. What are usually called "sailor-man's words" are almost exclusively English or Scandinavian or Dutch. Though the first Normans who settled in France gave up their own language, and the third generation spoke only French, many Norse words are found in the French nautical language, relics of the ancestral trade of Rollo and his fellows. It is safe to assume, however, that the vocabulary of the English sailor was not recruited from the Norman French, but is radically Anglo-Saxon or Danish. It is very extensive and almost destitute of any Latin element. The official terms of the navy, on the contrary, embrace many words of Romance origin. *Captain, lieutenant, commodore, commandant,* and *admiral* are not seamen's words. They would say, preferably, *skipper* or *mate* if they had invented the terms. The seamen's vocabulary is large, because a ship is a home to them in which they are isolated from the world for long periods, and because they have gathered words from foreign countries, like *catamaran* from Ceylon, *kedge* and *yawl* from the Dutch, and the local names of boats from whatever port they entered. The great body of their speech is English. To begin with, all parts of the ship and rigging — *hull, bow, waist, stern, deck, mast, sails, shrouds, ratlines, halyards, yards, sprit, boom, jib, leech, bits, tops, keel, garboard, larboard, starboard, scuppers, rudder, tiller, helm, cockswain, gig, cutter, launch, jolly-boat, taffrail, belaying-pin, hawser, fathom, cabin, barge* (Celtic), *galley, mess, bunk, wake, berth*—are of Teutonic origin, and a great many of them are used only by sailors. If we use *rudder*, or *helm*, for instance, in any other sense except as applied to a boat, we use the words metaphorically. Their antiquity as sailors' words is evident from this fact, and in this they differ from the moulders' words heretofore alluded to. The only words of Latin origin and of everyday use by sailors are *forecastle, compass, capstan, cable*, and *binnacle;* for though in realistic stories a sailor may talk about "going on a long vyage," a real sailor says, preferably a *cruise*. *Prow*, too, is a literary word never heard "on board ship." A *castle* was once built on the stern of war-ships and a *fore castle* in the bow, with the absurd idea of imitating a fort, and the word *forecastle* is now applied to the quarters of the crew. *Quarters* has crept in, too, from the Latin *quartarius*, a fourth part, hence a part set off for any definite purpose; but this is originally a man-of-war term. A *compass* is a scientific instrument, and received a Latin name, and *chronometer*—a later invention— was given a Greek name. The box in which the compass was kept was called a *binnacle*, from the Latin *habitaculum*, a little room. *Gimbals* is also Latin, and is from *gemini*, meaning the twin rings. *Cable* is a French word, but has never—except for chains—superseded in common use the regular English word, *hawser*. *Course* is also a Latin word and, strictly, means the angle which the vessel's track makes with the meridian. The application of the word *courses* to the main sails cannot be explained. *Davits* is said to be derived from *davus*, the Latin popular name for a slave (used something like our word *Jack*), but this derivation is purely conjectural. *Capstan* is French and Spanish, from a Greek root, and an *anchor* was used by the Romans. The Saxons drew their small ships on the beach and must have used the oars to keep off from a lee shore. The words connected with handling the anchor, however, are English, as the *bars*, the *pawls*, *catheads*, *to trip*, or *to fish*. A small anchor, too, has a Dutch name—a *kedge*.

The *bow* of a ship is connected with the Saxon *bog*, the root meaning an *arm*, hence the *shoulder*. The *bow* of a ship is its *shoulder*, and a *bowline* is so called because it is fastened to the *shoulder* of the sail. This word is from the same root as *bough*—an arm of a tree, and is entirely distinct from *bow*, the archer's weapon which comes from *bugen*, to bend.

The vocabulary of English seamen is therefore radically Teutonic. Its racy individual character and lack of formality testifies to its antiquity and independence of foreign terms, and to the original sufficiency of English for practical matters. Its phrases are strong and expressive, and would be absurdly feeble if translated into Latin equivalents. It embodies the maritime life and seafaring character of a vigorous, out-door race, and is well worth examining by any one who wishes to appreciate the directness and force of spoken English.* This brief sketch does not even outline the subject.

Inductions similar in general character can be drawn from the vocabulary of the still older occupation, farming. Genuine farmers' words are of the Teutonic stock. Many of them belong to the class of words evidently related in all the Aryan tongues, and were used in the remote past, when the Proto-Aryans, the parent stock of Celt, Greek, Latin, and Teuton, spoke the same language and formed one tribe. Such are the names of the domestic animals, and of the old implements and operations. *Horse, mare, cow, bull, ram, ewe,*

* An admirable Chaucerian word, *rote*, is preserved by American sailors. It means the confused sound of the sea breaking on a beach, heard at a distance, and seems now to be especially applicable to the sound heard inland. It can hardly be connected with *roar*.

plough, sickle, thresh, milk, are radical words. Even the parts of the modern plough, the *landside,* the *mould-board,* the *beam,* the *share,* are old English. The *clevis* and the *coulter* are Latin attachments. A farmer to-day never calls himself an *agriculturist.* He speaks of the *plough's tail,* an expression which is a survival from the time when the plough had but one handle, and is strictly *plough-stall.* A *stall* is a handle, a word allied to the root of *still,* a *stall* being that by which the implement is held firm. The root appears also in the word *headstall,* that by which a horse is held comparatively still. His *stall* in which he stands is another English word, from a different English root, but allied to the first and to the Latin *sto* through common relationship to the original root, STA. This word *stall* in the sense of handle is also used by farmers when they say "*stale* of a pitchfork." The word *flail* is given as from the Latin, *flagellum.* If this be true the Saxons must have threshed their grain in some different way—by the feet of oxen, like the Hebrews, for instance. At all events, there is no stain on the lineage of *thresh.* The name for the two parts of the flail—the *swingle* and the *staff*—are unmistakably Saxon.

The names of the grains, *barley, corn, wheat;* of the trees, *oak, beech, apple,* are also old. Some weeds and roots bear testimony in their names to the country from which they were introduced, like *beet, carrot, turnip, radish, potato*, and *pumpkin*, and show that the Anglo-Saxons never lived in a country where these were indigenous. In the names of the products of the soil a great deal of archaic history is embodied. The primitive operations are denoted by primitive words, or perhaps we should say that the use of a primitive name proves the things or operations so designated to be ancient. The soil of England has never been cultivated by men who spoke French, and so the rural dialect abounds in good, old Saxon words. Many survivals of the old stock of words can be found in New England, some of which have been lost in England. Modern inventions have so modified farming work that many of the old terms are passing out of use. This is notably the case with words used in the household industries of spinning and weaving, as practised fifty years ago.

Many handicraft words are of obscure origin, since they have but rarely been printed, and their pronunciation has become so modified from the primitive sounds that it is sometimes very difficult to conjecture the original derivation or connection. The technical language of the professions, on the other hand, was early committed to writing in many documents. All pleadings in law were written in Norman-French for a century after the Conquest, and even after the issue was made and the trial conducted in the new English, the judgment was entered in Latin. Law terms are, therefore, universally Latin, though the common law is an evolution of the English nation. Law terms of Latin origin, though they are not so barbarous as medical terms, have little force or simplicity, except the short ones, like *deed, judge, arrest, jury, court, suit, writ, warrant, mortgage,* and *summons,* which have become fully naturalized. Such words as *replevin, quo warranto, affidavit, demurrer, certiorari, rebutter, garnishee, mandamus, cestui que trust, feme-covert,* and their congeners, which make up nine-tenths of the legal dialect, betray their foreign origin too freely to allow their admission into the society of the old English words which we recognize as part of our mother-tongue. The artificial character of these words has, no doubt, contributed to the artificial and remote character of the science of the law, which, at least in an old work on pleading, seems to be concerned with a verbal system, and not to refer to real things. It is worth noticing that the officer with whom Englishmen come most in contact retained his Saxon title—*sheriff,* or *shire-reeve.* This retention of the English word for the legal executive is somewhat analogous to the assumption by the Duke of Normandy of the title, "King of England," instead of the French style, "*roi,*" or "*suzerain.*"

The class which may be designated as Church words, or the ecclesiastical terminology, is also exclusively classic—Latin or Greek—in origin, with the exception of the Saxon derivatives, like *righteousness, goodness, kindness, brotherly love, sin, wickedness, selfishness, meekness,* and a few others, which express the underlying elements of human character as opposed to formal theological conceptions like *piety, devotion, regeneration, repentance, faith,* and a host of other terms of Latin origin. This is as might be expected. The Church of Western Europe was originally a Latin Church. Its sacred books were in Latin or Greek. Its volumes of ecclesiastical law were in Latin. Words that refer to the organization are, of course, Latin, as are also words that belong to party differences in the Church. At the same time religion deals with the ultimate facts of human nature, and in the most corrupt periods there were to be found in the Church some earnest priests whose hearts yearned towards their fellow-men; who, like their Master, "had compassion on the multitude," and wished so to speak that they—in good old phrase—"might be understanded of the people." Chaucer's "poor parson" spoke English, though he is rather Latinized in his story of Melibœus, as Harry Bailey notices. We owe much to Wycliffe, Tyndale, Coverdale, and the seventeenth century revisers, that they translated the Bible into our mother-tongue, and not into Latinized English, and thereby gave their words a unique and radical power. The watchwords of the human systems over which men argue and fight, under the influence of that peculiarly Latin mental condition—"*odium theologicum*"—pass away and possess only a historical interest after a century or two. They are invariably Latin watchwords. The word *atonement*—at-one-ment—with its Saxon base and Latin suffix, is almost the only one of the theologic war-cries that is an exception to this rule, but this word embodies a concept as deep and abiding as that expressed by its correlative, *sin*, and is a word of an entirely different class from such strictly doctrinal words as *transubstantiation, predestination, election, eschatology*, etc.

The relations of the Classic and Saxon derivatives in theological nomenclature open too broad a field to be gone into at present, but it is worth while to consider the different effects of such phrases as "*an offended Deity*" and "*an angry God.*"

Just as chemistry retains some words which date back to the mediæval quackeries, alchemy and magic, and as astronomy retains some of the words once peculiar to the pseudo-science, astrology, so medicine shows traces of the terminology of the "learned leeches" of the Middle Ages. All medical books were then in Latin, and the mediæval names were kept in use even after Latin was discarded. They became a sort of professional shibboleth which gave mystery and dignity to simple matters. Even now the names of drugs are translated, and *dandelion* is mentioned as *taraxicum*, and *foxglove* as *digitalis*. For scientific classification special names are necessary, and Latin still offers the most convenient storehouse of words which have the same meaning in all countries. The doctors have an hereditary fondness for "words of learned length and thundering sound," and will hardly condescend to speak of the *backbone* or the *skull*. Like cooks, they are fond of giving foreign names to mysterious compounds. But the great object of their efforts—health—and the important events over which they preside—*childbirth* and *death*, which, indeed, concern the patient more than the physician—remain radically Saxon. The vocabulary peculiar to the profession testifies to the cosmopolitan nature of diseases and remedies. The world has been searched for the latter, and the former are common to men of all nations. Possibly it may testify to the fact that the wealthy Normans were more frequently the objects of the doctor's care than were the humbler Saxons. We have dropped the expressive Saxon *writh*—connected with *writhe*—and have retained the French equivalent, *fever*. Traces of the old medical notions can be discovered in medical words. *Cholera*, for instance, is derived through Latin from the Greek word meaning *bile*. *Gangrene*, from the same source, means something which gnaws. The fact that the Latins drew their notions of medical science from the Greeks is shown by the number of Greek - Latin and Greek derivatives in use among doctors. Of these are : *antiseptic, asthma, artery, bronchitis, cranium, œsophagus, epidermis, larynx, spleen, pleurisy, pore, rheum, surgeon*. We very early dropped the Saxon word *leech* in favor of the Latin *doctor*, or the Latin-Greek *physician*.

The vocabulary of mines is a curious jumble of archaic words—Celtic and Saxon—and modern scientific engineering terms. A classification of miners' words would prove very interesting and instructive.

That events could be foretold by an expert examination of the stars was a very general belief from the earliest time. In the Middle Ages the practice was reduced to rules, and gave rise to a precise technical vocabulary, which has left some curious traces in our language. We still use the words *horoscope* and *ill-starred* with a consciousness of their metaphorical force. But *consideration, disaster, aspect, contemplate,* and *influence* are habitually spoken without any thought of their origin. They are all astrological words, and, naturally, are of Greek or Latin derivation. *Consider* is *considerare*, to consult the *stars*. *Disaster* is an unpropitious position of a star. The sky was divided into temples or houses, and to *contemplate* was to examine what planets occupied the different temples at a given time. *Influence* is the occult power supposed to *flow* in from the moon or planets. *Aspect* meant the general relation of the planets and their distances from each other. Two planets could assume nine "*aspects*"— five good aspects and four bad ones—with which they looked on the earth—a slight fraction in favor of optimistic views. The planet which rose above the horizon at the hour of birth was said to be in the *ascendant*, and was supposed to exert a peculiar influence on the future life. *Conjunction* signifies that two planets were in the same temple, and we still use *conjunction* not only to mean a bond, but for two events happening about the same time. *Contemplate* dates back to Roman astrology, or even to Greek, since *templum* is from τέμνω, to cut, and is based on the idea of a place set apart or cut off. *Auspicious, avesspectare*, is from the Roman art of divination.

It is possible that some of these words, as *aspect* and *contemplate*, might have come into the language, even had they not formed a part of the vocabulary of mediæval astrology, but it is evident that their character has been affected by that use. The force of a word is affected by all its associations, and a knowledge of them enables us to appreciate precise and delicate uses of the word.

From the groups of folk-words, especially from the maritime and agricultural groups, the literary language is recruited. They are the living and vigorous roots of national speech, and pruning the upper growth without allowing the vital sap to circulate is futile; fortunately so, for if it were not, it would be criminal. The superiority of the words of the working trades over the words of the learned professions, in directness, force, and power of vividly presenting the thing signified, proves that a language, to possess any of these qualities, must be a growth, and not a "manufactured article."

ADDITIONAL WORDS FOR ILLUSTRATION.

Find the meaning of the word in the language from which it was taken into our modern English. Show the connection between the original meaning and the modern meaning. Use a modern dictionary.

Abbot.	Alms.
Abominate.	Ambergris.
Accord.	Ambidextrous.
Accost.	Amorphous.
Acid.	Appal.
Acorn.	Appraise.
Acquit.	Apprise.
Acute.	Apron.
Adequate.	Arch.
Adroit.	Ark.
Affidavit.	Arm.
Agate.	Attic.
Alarm.	Auction.
Alligator.	Aureole.
Allow.	Ballad.
Ally.	Ballet.

ADDITIONAL WORDS FOR ILLUSTRATION. 245

Ballot.
Ban.
Battledoor.
Battlement.
Between.
Bitter-end.
Blaze.
Blindfold.
Blunderbuss.
Bondsman.
Bower.
Brattice.
Buttress.
Buxom.
Calculate.
Cancel.
Cant.
Capitulate.
Caprice.
Cardinal.
Carnival.
Casemate.
Cat's-cradle.
Causeway.
Centering.
Chancellor.
Chaperon.
Chatter.
Chivalry.

Clever.
Collaborator.
Colonel.
Combat.
Commence.
Comparison.
Craven.
Cutter.
Dad.
Dainty.
Damsel.
Date.
Début.
Demure.
Deuce.
Dextrous.
Diamond.
Direct.
Ditty.
Dry (tedious).
Eagle.
Ear.
Ecstasy.
Elixir.
Ember-days.
Envelop.
Etch.
Expectorate.
Fanatic.

Fare.
February.
Fend.
Ferry.
Fit.
Founder.
Friday.
Fritter.
Frontispiece.
Gantlet.
Gingerly.
Goggle-eyed.
Guinea.
Gutta-percha.
Halyard.
Hammer-cloth.
Hanger.
Hematite.
Hollyhock.
Humble-pie
Husband.
Infantry.
Instep.
January.
Jerked beef.
Jet.
Jot.
Kernel.
Kickshaw.

Kindle.
Laconic.
Lasso.
Lawn.
Left.
Lieutenant.
Limb (of the Sun).
Linstock.
Listless.
Loathsome.
Manœuvre.
Map.
March.
Martyr.
Maundy-Thursday.
Metre.
Mildew.
Mob.
Mosaic.
Muse (vb).
Napkin.
Nation.
Nightmare.
Normal.
Observe.
Obstinate.
Old Nick.
Onion.
Oriole.

ADDITIONAL WORDS FOR ILLUSTRATION. 247

Pale.
Palette.
Pallid.
Parboil.
Parson.
Patent.
Pathos.
Patient.
Pea-jacket.
Pedant.
Peer.
Pendulum.
Pew.
Plumb.
Pope.
Posy.
Press-gang.
Prophesy.
Provender.
Pulley.
Punch (vb).
Purblind.
Purée (a soup).
Purloin.
Pusillanimous.
Pyramid.
Queen (in chess).
Quit.
Rant.

Recount.
Reindeer.
Remark.
Restive.
Rook (in chess).
Rote.
Rout.
Route.
Rut.
Sarcophagus.
Seminary.
Sentry.
Sinister.
Skeleton.
Smoke (to find out).
Soldier.
Soprano.
Steelyard.
String (of horses).
Supplant.
Tangle (sea-weed).
Tantalize.
Termagant.
Testament.
Thursday.
Thwarts.
Tontine.
Touchy.
Train-oil.

Traitor.
Tribulation.
Trick (at cards).
Trigger.
Tuesday.
Tureen.
Uncouth.
Vermilion.
Vinegar.
Volume.
Walnut.

Wardrobe.
Wednesday.
Welcome.
Welsh-rabbit.
Whiskey.
Wiseacre.
Worsted.
Wound (a horn).
Yankee.
Zero.
Zodiac.

INDEX OF SUBJECTS.

Anglo-Saxon terminations, 78.
"Ar," the root, 181.
Arnold, Matthew, quotation, 88.
Aryan stock, 13.
Aryans, home of, 13.
—— languages of, 31.
Astrologers' words, 241.

Berners, Juliana, quotation, 66.
Bible, translations of, 60–83.
Blacksmiths' words, 217.
Book of St. Albans, 65.
Branching of words, 129.
Britain abandoned by Romans, 37.
—— invaded by Saxons, 38.
Browning, quotation, 144.
Brugmann's classification, 20.
Builders' words, 224.

Change from Anglo-Saxon to English, 43.
Chivalry, language of, 63.
Collect, quotation from, 91.
Colloquial English, 47.

Composite character of English, 91.
Concrete images in language, 119.
Critic, quotation from, 150.

Danish invasion, 40.
Dialectic English, 48.
Dialects, 40.
Doctors' words, 239.
Double names, 180.
Double rhymes, 85.

Earle's Philology, quotation, 25.
Ecclesiastical words, 238.
Effect of material surroundings, 123.
Emerson, quotation from, 94.
English, changes in, 37–49.
—— kinds of, 47.
—— Latin element in, 56.
—— Norse element in, 98.
—— number of words in, 92.
—— rhythm of, 44.
—— sources of, 36.
Erroneous derivations, 140.
Etymologies promote good use, 92.

Euphemism, 166.
Euphuism, 68.

FARMERS' words, 234.
Founders' words, 229.
Fourteenth century poem, 42.
Fuller, Dr. Thos., quotation, 140.

GRIMM'S Law, 25–28.

HALE, Horatio, quotation, 33.
Hunting, language of, 64.
Hybrid words, 93.

IMITATIVE words, 123.
Invasion of Britain, 37.
Ivanhoe, quotation, 70.

KINDS of English, 47.
Kitchen words, 52.

LANGUAGE, Albanian, 20.
—— a mark of humanity, 1–3.
—— Anglo-Saxon, 19.
—— Armenian, 20.
—— branches of study of, 9.
—— Celtic, 16–55.
—— classification of, 13.
—— connection with thought, 4.
—— Cornish, 16.
—— Cymric, 16.
—— Dutch, 19.
—— Friesic, 19.
—— Gallic, 20.
—— German, 18.
—— Gothic, 18.
—— Hellenic, 16.
—— High German, 18.
—— how far an evolution, 7.

Language, Indian branch of, 15.
—— Indo-European, 13.
—— Iranian, 15.
—— Italic, 17.
—— Low German, 19.
—— Netherlandish, 19.
—— Norse, 18.
—— Old English, 19.
—— origin of, 113.
—— Platt-Deutsch, 19.
—— Romance, group of, 17.
—— Slavonic, 16.
—— Teutonic, 18.
—— Welsh, 16.
Latin element in English, 56.
Law words, 237.
Literary English, 47.
London slang, 53.

MAX MÜLLER, quotation, 31–47, 92.
Miners' words, 241.
Modern scientific words, 126.
Monosyllables, French, 81.
Morte d'Arthur, 65.

NAMES, corrupted from French, 173.
—— double ethnic, 178–180.
—— European place, 178.
—— history in, 170.
—— Indian, 171.
—— modified in sound, 173.
—— New England place, 175.
—— North American, 172.
—— of birds, 122.
—— of Connecticut towns, 175.
—— of rivers, 184.
—— Southern place, 176.
—— Spanish, 172–174.

INDEX OF SUBJECTS. 251

Nicknames, 204.
Norman conquest, 61.
—— invasion, 41.
Norse element in English, 98.
Number of words in English, 92.

ONOMATOPŒIA, 124.
Origin of language, 113.

PAIRS of words, 73–76.
Periods of Latin introduction, 57.
Poetic quality of words, 88.
Poetry in words, 118.
Printers' words, 221.
Pronunciation (note), 30.
Proportion of Latin, 108.
Public, or ordinary English, 47.

RHYMES, 84.
Root "ar," 181.

SAILORS' words, 231.
Sanskrit, 32.
Set, 183.
Shakspeare, quotation, 89, 90, 144.
Shoemakers' words, 222.
Sir Tristram, 65.
Skeat's Dictionary, 92.
Slang, 50–53.
Spelling, 29–155.
St. Albans, Book of, 65.
Steam-engine, 220.
Suffixes, 97.
Surnames from personal traits, 210.
—— increase of, 212.
—— local, 205.

Surnames, occupative, 208.
—— percentage, 212.
—— total number of, 213.
Synonyms, 74.

WORDS, Arabic, 102.
—— branching of, 129.
—— builders', 224.
—— Celtic, 46–51.
—— changes in meaning, 158.
—— character of Romance, 87.
—— Dutch, 106.
—— expressing mental states, 120.
—— founded on metaphors, 115.
—— Greek, 107.
—— Hebrew, 105.
—— hunting, 66.
—— hybrid, 93.
—— imitative, 123.
—— kitchen, 52.
—— Latin, 56.
—— modern scientific, 126.
—— Norman-French, 72.
—— Norse, 98.
—— of astrology, 241.
—— of the trades, 222.
—— pairs of, 77.
—— per cent. of Latin, 108.
—— poetry in, 118.
—— printers', 221.
—— professional, 237.
—— record changes of thought, 169.
—— rhythm of English, 44.
—— sailors', 231.
—— society, 66.
—— value of study of, 5.

INDEX OF WORDS AND EXPRESSIONS EXPLAINED.

Abominable, 141.
Acorn, 152.
Admiral, 104.
Adventurer, 166.
Affront, 161.
Agere, 137.
Alchemy, 103.
Alcohol, 103.
Alembic, 103.
Algebra, 103.
Alkali, 103.
Allow, 165.
Alms, 59.
Amazement, 165.
Amazon, 141.
Ambition, 160.
Ampersand, 166.
Andiron, 152.
Anse de Cousins, 149.
Antic, 160.
Apace, 152.
Apostle, 59.
Ascendant, 242.
Aspect, 242.
Atonement, 239.
Attention, 119.
Auspicious, 242.
Average, 163.
Aye, 99.

Baggage, 51.
Baie de Lièvre, 173.
Baie des Espoirs, 173.
Bailey, 59.
Barker, 209.
Beak, 53.
Beatan, 138.

Beefsteak, 133.
Belfry, 164.
Bellerophon, 147.
Beorgan, 138.
Binnacle, 233.
Bishop, 59.
Blawan, 138.
Boblo, 173.
Bois Blanc, 173.
Bottom, 206.
Bound, 99.
Bow, 233.
Bowline, 233.
Brace, 64.
Brash, 226.
Brick, 53.
Brown Willy, 149.
Brynen, 138.
Bud, 119.
Bunker, 210.
Burne, 206.
Business, 167.
Butler, 208.
Bye, 101.

Calc, 59.
Calipers, 168.
Candidate, 160.
Canter, 168.
Carmine, 73.
Carpenter, 51.
Castra, 57.
Ceapian, 138.
Cester, 57.
"Cheese it," 53.
Chester, 58.
Cholera, 241.

WORDS AND EXPRESSIONS EXPLAINED. 253

Church, 60.
Cinder, 218.
Cipher, 104.
Clerc, 59.
Clough, 206.
Cobb, 206.
Cobbler, 222.
Cock, 153.
Colonia, 58.
Combe, 205.
Compassion, 120.
Compliment, 140.
Comprehension, 120.
Conception, 119.
Condign, 152.
Conjunction, 242.
Consider, 242.
Contemplate, 242.
Courage, 120.
Course, 233.
Court-cards, 147.
Crank, 128.
Crayfish, 147.
Credo, 137.
Crimson, 73.
Crouch, 206.
Crucible, 229.
Cunning garth, 147.
Curmudgeon, 143.

DAISY, 118.
Dandelion, 147.
Davits, 233.
Dead Man, 149.
Defy, 137.
Den, 205.
Depart, 165.
Devil, 147.
Dico, 137.
Dilapidated, 11.
Dirge, 164.
Disaster, 242.
Do, 136.

Dog-cheap, 153.
Dozy, 226.
Drunk, 167.
Duco, 136.

EQUIPAGE, 143.
Ey, 206.

FAST, 99.
Fiery, 123.
Fiord, 101.
Fitful Head, 147.
Flag, 99.
Flail, 235.
Ford, 206.
Forecastle, 232.
Fork, 72.
Frank, 158.
Free, 159.
Freemantle, 210.
Frontispiece, 137.

GAL, 179.
Gambler, 166.
Gangrene, 241.
Geranium, 118.
Ghost, 116.
Gibraltar, 104.
Gimbals, 233.
God, 147.
Græci, 181.
Grammercy Park, 148.

HABERDASHER, 147.
Hadlyme, 175.
Hagenes, 150.
Hale, 99.
Ham, 207.
Hangnail, 148.
Harwinton, 175.
Hash, 227.
Hatch, 227.
Hate, 120.

Hayward, 209.
Hessians, 148.
Himalaya, 118.
Hirondelle, 147.
Holt, 206.
"Hook it," 53.
Howard, 209.
Humanities, 160.

IBRAHIM PASHA, 147.
Idea, 120.
Incentive, 149.
Influence, 242.
Ink, 221.
Insult, 161.

JERUSALEM, 148.
Jointer, 228.

"KICK the bucket," 53.
Kidder, 208.
King, 147.

LAST, 223.
Latimer, 208.
Lea, 205.
Leash, 65.
Legend, 145.
Le Tour Sans Venin, 148.
Loony, 122.
Lunacy, 122.
Ly, 206.
Lynch, 206.

MAGDEBURG, 149.
Maidenhead, 149.
Maidstone, 149.
Mallow, 118.
Mariposa, 142.
Marquis, 69.
Marshall, 69.
Masher, 53.
Maul-stick, 147.

Memory, 121.
Modest, 120.
Much, 143.

NASTURTIUM, 119.
Nice, 162.
Noble, 69.
Nott, 210.

OLD Man, 149.

PALMER, 209.
Panther, 144.
Passion, 120.
Peel, 210.
Phantomnation, 150.
Picketwire, 173.
Pie, 142.
Pigeon English, 167.
Pilatus, Mount, 145.
Pilgrim, 209.
Pink, 118.
Plaid, 52.
Plough's tail, 235.
Policy, 163.
Pomfret, 174.
Porter, 209.
Pose, 131.
Post, 131.
Posthumous, 164.
Prairie, Dippertree, 173.
Precipitate, 10.
Preface, 137.
Presbyter, 59.
Priest, 59.

QUAD, 221.
Quadrangle, 131.
Quadrille, 131.
Quadroon, 131.
Quadruped, 131.
Quaint, 162.
Quarry, 64, 131.

WORDS AND EXPRESSIONS EXPLAINED.

Quart, 131.
Quarters, 232.
Quarto, 131.

RENCONTRE, 173.
Rive, 228.
Romance, 160.
Rosemary, 118.
Ross, 206.
Russell, 210.

SACKSMITH, 208.
Sale, 206.
Salt-cellar, 143.
Score, 135.
Scudder, 208.
Scutcheon, 63.
Shaw, 205.
Shear, 135.
Sheriff, 237.
Shirt, 135.
Shuttle-cock, 147.
Sirloin, 152.
Skilagalee, 173.
Slag, 218.
Slang, 127.
Slug-horn, 144.
Smith, 217.
Soo, 173.
Sparrow-grass, 147.
Spend, 165.
Spirit, 116.
Splay, 165.
Sport, 165.
Squad, 131.
Squadron, 131.
Stack, 133.
Stake, 133.
Stall, 235.
Stamwick, 175.
Stick, 132.
Stock, 133.
Stoker, 133.

Stone-blind, 143.
St. Oreste, 150.
Strata, 58.
Stratfield, 175.
Street, 58.
Stunt, 226.
Surly, 152.
Surround, 161.
Sutherland, 118.
Swell, 128.
Sykes, 206.
Sympathy, 120.

TALENTS, 121.
Tango, 136.
Tap, 224.
Tarpaulin, 162.
Tartars, 140, 148.
Temper, 121.
Temperature, 121.
Think, 121.
Thorp, 205.
Tick, 132.
Ticket, 132.
Ton, 207.
Trivial, 161.
Twig, 53.

UPSTART, 151.

VALLUM, 58.
Venison, 64.
WEAL, 53.
Welch, 53.
Welcher, 179.
Whole, 99.
Wintonbury, 175.
Wormwood, 154.
Writh, 240.
Writhe, 240.
Wylen, 53.

ZERO, 104.

www.ingramcontent.com/pod-product-compliance
Lightning Source LLC
Chambersburg PA
CBHW021349230426
43666CB00006B/462